Grammar and Punctuation

Career Step, LLC
Phone: 801.489.9393
Toll-Free: 800.246.7837
Fax: 801.491.6645
careerstep.com

This text companion contains a snapshot of the online program content converted to a printed format. Please note that the online training program is constantly changing and improving and is always the source of the most up-to-date information.

Product Number: HG-PR-11-090
Generation Date: March 16, 2011

Table of Contents

Unit 1
Introduction

Introduction to Grammar and Punctuation

Learning Objective

This module is a refresher of basic English grammar and punctuation rules. Upon completion, the student will be able to recognize and identify proper usage, language, punctuation, and spelling.

One very important skill required for any job is a working knowledge of English grammar. You need to know how to construct a proper sentence with the correct employment of usage, capitalization, and punctuation. Thus, it is essential that you be familiar and comfortable with the basic rules of English grammar.

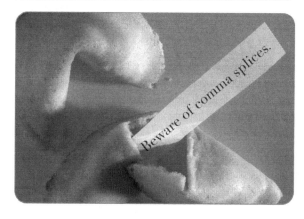

This module on grammar is designed to be a refresher course. You probably studied English in school, and this is intended as a review of some of those rules. You will have opportunities to practice and apply each element as you review it. Don't hesitate to spend longer on rules that may not be as familiar to you or that you need help with. As is the case throughout the program, you will be tested at the end of each unit. Your scores should never be less than 85% before going on to other units.

Unit 2
Parts of Speech

Parts of Speech – Introduction

Unless you are an English teacher or you learned English as a second language, you probably don't spend a lot of time thinking about the types and functions of the words you use when you speak. We tend to simply internalize the rules of the English language when we learn to speak. Then, through repetitive practice we learn to build sentences correctly (usually). However, an "organic" knowledge of the English language is not enough. To be professionally accurate, you must know the basics as well as the advanced rules governing the language. So in our effort to review and re-acquaint you with the rules of grammar and punctuation, we will start with the basics: the parts of speech.

You probably have not thought about the parts of speech since you diagrammed sentences in high school. While that was excellent and effective practice, we are going to forgo formal diagramming and focus on the **roles** the parts of speech play in building good sentences.

While anyone can memorize the definitions of the parts of speech (there are only eight of them), knowing the definitions does not do any good unless you can understand the function of the parts of speech within a sentence. It is imperative that you understand the function of individual words because they are the basic building blocks of our complex language. Good words make good phrases and clauses, which make good sentences, which make good paragraphs, and therefore great writing… and that, after all, is your goal!

Parts of Speech

Without further ado, let's re-introduce you to the eight parts of speech:

Noun: Word used to name a person, place, thing, or idea.

Pronoun: Word used in place of a noun.

Adjective: Word used to modify a noun or a pronoun.

Verb: Word that expresses action or shows a state of being.

Adverb: Word used to modify a verb, adjective, or other adverb.

Preposition: Word that shows the relation of a noun to another word in the sentence.

Conjunction: Word that joins other words/groups of words.

Interjection: Word that adds emotion to a sentence (Wow!). Since these are almost never used in professional writing, we will not spend time on interjections.

The way each part of speech behaves in a sentence and its interaction with the other words in the sentence is what forms clear, correct sentences. Many of the words in our language can be more than one part of speech. You must know the word's role in the sentence to understand what part of speech it is in that particular instance.

> The child would **scream** every time she lost her blanket.
> The mother heard a **scream** coming from her daughter's room.

> *In the first sentence, **scream** is an action—a verb.*
> *In the second sentence, **scream** is a thing—a noun.*
>
> *Only by understanding the function of the word and those surrounding it would you be able to know what part of speech the word is.*

The nice thing about this unit is that you are familiar with the information because you build sentences every time you speak or write. All we are doing is naming and explaining that which you already know.

Nouns and Pronouns

Nouns are words that represent people, places, things, or ideas.

   People: brother, minister, wife, Nancy Reagan, teacher, Abraham Lincoln

   Place: school, Earth, store, New Mexico, home

   Thing: table, chicken, leg, Washington Monument, chewing gum, Toyota truck

   Idea: love, honor, fear, anger, hatred

Nouns that are capitalized are called **proper nouns**. They point out specific people, places, or things. Nouns that are not capitalized are called **common nouns**.

Nouns can come anywhere in a sentence—the beginning, middle, or end.

> I'm taking my **dog** to the **kennel** in late **February**.
>
> *February is a proper noun. **Dog** and **kennel** are common nouns.*
>
> I miss **Florida** because we would get **sunshine** throughout the **winter**.
>
> *Florida is a proper noun. **Sunshine** and **winter** are common nouns.*
>
> She said her **jealousy** for **Abbey** started as a little **thing** and grew into a **monster**.
>
> *Abbey is a proper noun. **Jealousy**, **thing**, and **monster** are common nouns.*

Remember the idea of looking at a word's **function** in the sentence rather than just the definition of the particular part of speech. A word that is a noun can also be used to describe another noun. The word is then considered an adjective because of its function in the sentence.

> The **patient** has a **history** of colon **cancer**.
>
> *Although **colon** is a noun (a thing), in this case it is modifying the word **cancer**. It would be considered an adjective in this sentence.*
>
> She complains of joint **pain** in her left **elbow**.
>
> *Again, **joint** is usually a noun. In this case, it modifies the word **pain**, so it is considered an adjective.*

A **pronoun** is a word that takes the place of a noun. We use pronouns because our sentences would become long, redundant, and confusing if we only used nouns.

Janet's daughter brought Janet's daughter's lunch to Janet's daughter's first day of kindergarten.

Help! We need pronouns!

Janet's daughter brought **her** lunch to **her** first day of kindergarten.

Whew. Much better.

There are many types of pronouns, but all of them have one thing in common: they replace a noun. While you will not be expected to identify each of the different types of pronouns, they will be explained here so you can see the functions they have within different sentences.

Who ate **mine**?

Who *is an interrogative pronoun (pronoun used to ask a question). It takes the place of the person who ate the food. The other interrogative pronouns are* **which, what**, *and* **whom**.

Mine *is a possessive pronoun that takes the place of the speaker and shows his/her ownership of the food (before someone ate it, of course). The other possessive pronouns are* **yours, hers, his, its, ours, whose,** *and* **theirs**. *If they precede a noun, they are* **my, your, her, his, their, its, our, whose**.

This is too heavy for **me**.

This *takes the place of whatever the thing is that is heavy. It is a demonstrative pronoun, which points to a thing or person. The other demonstrative pronouns are* **that, these,** *and* **those**.

Me *is a personal pronoun—the most common kind. It takes the place of a person. The other personal pronouns are* **I, you, he, she, it, we, they, her, him, it, us, them**. *Of course, they change forms depending upon the number and gender of the people they replace.*

Everything John found was returned to the person **who** lost it.

Everything *takes place of all of the items John found. This is called an indefinite pronoun because it replaces things/people that are not specific. Some other indefinite pronouns are* **everyone, anyone, someone, any, all, few, many, none, nobody, somebody**.

Who *is a relative pronoun in this case. A relative pronoun relates to a noun that precedes it in the sentence. It connects a dependent clause to the noun that it relates to. In this sentence* **who** *relates to* **person** *(and connects* **who lost it** *to the person). These are probably the most difficult pronouns to identify. The other relative pronouns are* **whoever, which, that, whom, and whomever.**.

Challenge Box

Test yourself on these sentences. What are the pronouns in the following sentences?

1. What did she call you?
2. Everyone was invited to her party.
3. Only the wealthiest customers pay for these.
4. The plane that landed here lost its landing gear.
5. Nobody will know if we simply replace the window that cracked.

Adjectives

If you have ever known someone who loves to work on cars, you may have seen them modify the automobile in some way. Perhaps they added a new exhaust system or changed the stereo or even painted the body of the car... all of those are examples of **modifying** a car. Similarly, the job of an adjective is to **modify** a noun or pronoun. To modify a noun, an **adjective** can describe the noun, add more information about it, or quantify it. An adjective will answer one of the following three questions about the noun it modifies:

The *red* apple

1. Which one?
2. What kind?
3. How many?

The boy went down the **red slide**.

> The adjective **red** modifies the noun **slide** by telling **what color** the slide was.

She ate **two hamburgers** for lunch.

> The adjective **two** modifies the noun **hamburgers** by telling **how many** hamburgers.

We told him to bring his purchase back to **this store** to get a full refund.

> The adjective **this** modifies the noun **store** by telling **which store**.

> *Note—Remember the word **this** was also a pronoun when used by itself in a sentence. It is an adjective when it precedes a noun because it modifies the noun. It's all about the **function** of the word!*

Possessive pronouns can also be used as adjectives. When they modify a noun or pronoun, they are functioning as an adjective rather than a pronoun.

She was asked to raise **her hand**.

> *Since the word **her** is modifying the noun **hand** by telling **which hand**, it is considered an adjective.*

Remember the interrogative pronouns (those that ask a question)? They can also function as adjectives. Just look at the function of the word in the sentence.

Which dog barked the loudest?

*The word **which** modifies the noun **dog** by telling (or in this case, asking) which dog.*

I. **MULTIPLE CHOICE.**
The following sentences have some nouns, pronouns, and adjectives which are in orange. Choose the correct part of speech for each orange word. If it is an adjective, enter the noun that it modifies in the box provided.

She wanted to go to the **shoe store** at the **new** mall.

1. **She**
   - ○ noun
   - ○ pronoun
   - ○ adjective. What noun does it modify? _____

2. **shoe**
   - ○ noun
   - ○ pronoun
   - ○ adjective. What noun does it modify? _____

3. **store**
   - ○ noun
   - ○ pronoun
   - ○ adjective. What noun does it modify? _____

4. **new**
   - ○ noun
   - ○ pronoun
   - ○ adjective. What noun does it modify? _____

The **man** wanted to see **his oldest son** that weekend.

5. **man**
   - ○ noun
   - ○ pronoun
   - ○ adjective. What noun does it modify? _____

6. **his**
   - ○ noun
   - ○ pronoun
   - ○ adjective. What noun does it modify? _____

7. **oldest**
   - ◯ noun
   - ◯ pronoun
   - ◯ adjective. What noun does it modify? _____

8. **son**
   - ◯ noun
   - ◯ pronoun
   - ◯ adjective. What noun does it modify? _____

The person **who** could eat the most **spicy** chili dogs would be the **winner**.

9. **who**
   - ◯ noun
   - ◯ pronoun
   - ◯ adjective. What noun does it modify? _____

10. **spicy**
    - ◯ noun
    - ◯ pronoun
    - ◯ adjective. What noun does it modify? _____

11. **winner**
    - ◯ noun
    - ◯ pronoun
    - ◯ adjective. What noun does it modify? _____

The **old rusty** car sat in the middle of an empty **field**.

12. **old**
    - ◯ noun
    - ◯ pronoun
    - ◯ adjective. What noun does it modify? _____

13. **rusty**
    - ◯ noun
    - ◯ pronoun
    - ◯ adjective. What noun does it modify? _____

14. **field**
    - ◯ noun
    - ◯ pronoun
    - ◯ adjective. What noun does it modify? _____

The **wooden** chest **she** found was unfortunately **empty**.

15. **wooden**
   - ○ noun
   - ○ pronoun
   - ○ adjective. What noun does it modify? _____

16. **she**
   - ○ noun
   - ○ pronoun
   - ○ adjective. What noun does it modify? _____

17. **empty**
   - ○ noun
   - ○ pronoun
   - ○ adjective. What noun does it modify? _____

The **salt** had spilled across the **dirty** tabletop.

18. **salt**
   - ○ noun
   - ○ pronoun
   - ○ adjective. What noun does it modify? _____

19. **dirty**
   - ○ noun
   - ○ pronoun
   - ○ adjective. What noun does it modify? _____

Verbs

The **verb** is the most important part of speech because a sentence cannot exist without it. It is the only part of speech that is essential to a sentence. You can have a sentence without a noun or an adjective or a pronoun, but you cannot have a sentence without a verb. Why not? Simply put, the verb acts like the engine of a car—it makes the sentence "go." A **verb** gives action to or expresses the state of being of the thing (noun or pronoun) the sentence is about.

> The woman **fell** from her porch several days ago.
>
> *The word **fell** gives action to the noun **woman**. Without the verb, this would not be a sentence.*
>
> He **stretches** every morning.
>
> *The verb **stretches** gives action to the pronoun **he**.*

In addition to showing action, verbs can show a state of being. The verbs that show state of being are called **linking verbs**. They link the noun or pronoun to another word (usually an adjective or another noun).

The man **is** a cashier.

*The verb **is** links the noun **man** to the noun **cashier**, showing us the state of the patient.*

She **seems** content with the current program.

*The verb **seems** links the pronoun **she** to the adjective **content**, showing us the state of this female.*

*The most common linking verbs are the verbs of being: **be, been, being, is, am, are, was, were.***

*There are other verbs that are commonly used as linking verbs: **become, seem, appear, look, feel.***

Verbs can change forms depending upon the number of the nouns or pronouns that they are giving action to or linking.

The man **goes** to the office.

But

Two men **go** to the office.

We will cover this in detail in a future unit on agreement. But verbs can also change form depending upon tense. Many times, it will take a compound verb to accurately express tense. A **compound verb** is simply a main verb plus one or more helping verbs.

He **will be going** to visit his sister in Maine soon.

***Going** is the main verb, and the helping verbs **will** and **be** express a specific tense (in this case the simple future tense).*

They **were skiing** when the accident occurred.

***Skiing** is the main verb and **were** is the helping verb. Combined they give us a specific tense (in this case the past progressive tense).*

She **will** not **be** happy when she sees her favorite cup broken.

Sometimes the compound verb is split by an adverb (not, never, finally, etc.) They are NOT part of the verb.

Challenge Box

Test yourself on these sentences. Identify the verbs and see if you can tell if they are linking verbs or action verbs.

1. He will call us in a week's time.
2. Over the next several days, she received several congratulations on her engagement.
3. Because he does not have enough soda, I will send someone to the store.
4. He appeared happy when he spoke to us.
5. She looks good and will follow up if things change for the worse.

Adverbs

An adverb is commonly used to modify an adjective, another adverb, or a verb. If modifying a verb, it can tell **how**, **when**, **where**, or **to what extent** (how often or how much) the action is done.

> He drives **carefully**. (how)
> He drives **early**. (when)
> He can **almost** drive. (to what extent, how much)
> He drives **everywhere**. (where)

Adverbs such as *actually, indeed, truly,* and *really* that modify verbs can also be used for emphasis.

> She can **really** sing.
> He is **indeed** happy.

An adverb can also modify an adjective.

> He is a **really** good driver.*
> The patient was **desperately** afraid of facing surgery.
> It was an **abnormally** high fever.
>
> > ***Really*** *modifies the adjective* ***good****, as in "really good," not the noun "driver" (really driver?). If it were modifying the verb in this sentence, it would have to read, "He really is a good driver."*

An adverb can also modify another adverb.

> He performed **very** well.
>
> > ***Very*** *modifies* ***well****, which is an adverb because it modifies the verb* ***performed****: he performed well.*

Occasionally a word can function as either a noun or an adverb.

> He was tired **yesterday**. (adverb)
> She will be discharged **tomorrow**. (adverb)

I think I will go **today**. (adverb)
Today is the first day of the rest of your life. (noun)
Yesterday was a lousy day. (noun)
Tomorrow will be worse. (noun)

In the following sentences, the adverb is highlighted and an arrow points to the word or words it modifies.

1. He eventually **moved** out of his brother's basement.

2. She **ate** quickly so she wouldn't be late.

3. He **became** progressively more ill.

4. The dog **chewed** happily on the bone.

5. I watched the sun **sink** slowly into the sea.

6. The gambler ultimately **lost** all his money.

7. The child **screamed** angrily.

8. He usually can **walk** and **exercise** and is quite vigorous.

9. He initially **thought** he didn't need any help on the project.

10. She gradually **understood** the process as she studied.

Adverbs in Action

The adverbs in the following examples function to specify time, place, intensity, and position.

We **often** take walks with our dog.
He **rarely** gets to work on time.
Put it right **there**.
Here comes your sister.
However you beg, you can't have another candy bar.
She **first** discovered her talent for drawing when she was five.
We are **never** home after 9 am.
He **always** rides his bike to school.
Unfortunately, she didn't get to the bus stop on time.

I. **MULTIPLE CHOICE.**
For each sentence choose the word that is an adverb.

1. We immediately called 911.
   - ○ We
   - ○ immediately
   - ○ called
   - ○ 911

2. The man spoke normally.
   - ○ The
   - ○ man
   - ○ spoke
   - ○ normally

3. The girl is somewhat hesitant.
   - ○ girl
   - ○ is
   - ○ somewhat
   - ○ hesitant

4. The dog was unusually lethargic.
   - ○ dog
   - ○ was
   - ○ unusually
   - ○ lethargic

5. She donates to the charity yearly.
   - ○ donates
   - ○ to
   - ○ charity
   - ○ yearly

II. **FILL IN THE BLANK.**
Each sentence below has an adverb highlighted. Enter into the blank which word or words the adverb modifies.

1. We decided to leave **tomorrow**.

   tomorrow modifies which word: _____

2. He went **immediately** to his office.

immediately modifies which word: _____

3. She had **definitely** watched too much TV.

   definitely modifies which word: _____

4. His condition deteriorated **rapidly**.

   rapidly modifies which word: _____

5. She **grossly** misjudged how much flour the cake would need.

   grossly modifies which word: _____

Review: Parts of Speech

I. **MULTIPLE CHOICE.**
   Choose the part of speech for each numbered word. (Pay attention to each word's function.) In the case of adjectives, enter the word(s) that they modify in the space beside the choice "adjective." For greater accuracy in scoring, be sure to type the words exactly as they appear, without extra spaces, and with no following or preceding punctuation.

The young[1] boy walked slowly[2] along the beach[3]. He dug his toes into the sand[4] and unearthed[5] a cracked[6] seashell. He rinsed[7] it in the waves[8] and noticed it[9] was very[10] smooth. His mother was calling[11] to him loudly[12], and he ran quickly[13] back, waving the seashell[14]. His younger[15] sister tried to grab it, but he[16] kept it out of her[17] reach. She began to cry[18], so the boy kindly[19] took her hand. They[20] walked across the beach until they found[21] another beautiful[22] seashell. The girl smiled[23] happily[24], and they returned to their mother[25].

1. **young**
   - ○ noun
   - ○ pronoun
   - ○ adjective. What noun does it modify? _____
   - ○ verb
   - ○ adverb

2. **slowly**
   - ○ noun
   - ○ pronoun
   - ○ adjective. What noun does it modify? _____
   - ○ verb
   - ○ adverb

3. **beach**

   ○ noun

   ○ pronoun

   ○ adjective. What noun does it modify? _____

   ○ verb

   ○ adverb

4. **sand**

   ○ noun

   ○ pronoun

   ○ adjective. What noun does it modify? _____

   ○ verb

   ○ adverb

5. **unearthed**

   ○ noun

   ○ pronoun

   ○ adjective. What noun does it modify? _____

   ○ verb

   ○ adverb

6. **cracked**

   ○ noun

   ○ pronoun

   ○ adjective. What noun does it modify? _____

   ○ verb

   ○ adverb

7. **rinsed**

   ○ noun

   ○ pronoun

   ○ adjective. What noun does it modify? _____

   ○ verb

   ○ adverb

8. **waves**

   ○ noun

   ○ pronoun

   ○ adjective. What noun does it modify? _____

   ○ verb

   ○ adverb

9. **it**

    ○ noun
    ○ pronoun
    ○ adjective. What noun does it modify? _____
    ○ verb
    ○ adverb

10. **very**

    ○ noun
    ○ pronoun
    ○ adjective. What noun does it modify? _____
    ○ verb
    ○ adverb

11. **was calling**

    ○ noun
    ○ pronoun
    ○ adjective. What noun does it modify? _____
    ○ verb
    ○ adverb

12. **loudly**

    ○ noun
    ○ pronoun
    ○ adjective. What noun does it modify? _____
    ○ verb
    ○ adverb

13. **quickly**

    ○ noun
    ○ pronoun
    ○ adjective. What noun does it modify? _____
    ○ verb
    ○ adverb

14. **seashell**

    ○ noun
    ○ pronoun
    ○ adjective. What noun does it modify? _____
    ○ verb
    ○ adverb

15. **younger**

   ○ noun
   ○ pronoun
   ○ adjective. What noun does it modify? _____
   ○ verb
   ○ adverb

16. **he**

   ○ noun
   ○ pronoun
   ○ adjective. What noun does it modify? _____
   ○ verb
   ○ adverb

17. **her**

   ○ noun
   ○ pronoun
   ○ adjective. What noun does it modify? _____
   ○ verb
   ○ adverb

18. **cry**

   ○ noun
   ○ pronoun
   ○ adjective. What noun does it modify? _____
   ○ verb
   ○ adverb

19. **kindly**

   ○ noun
   ○ pronoun
   ○ adjective. What noun does it modify? _____
   ○ verb
   ○ adverb

20. **They**

   ○ noun
   ○ pronoun
   ○ adjective. What noun does it modify? _____
   ○ verb
   ○ adverb

21. **found**
    - ◯ noun
    - ◯ pronoun
    - ◯ adjective. What noun does it modify? _____
    - ◯ verb
    - ◯ adverb

22. **beautiful**
    - ◯ noun
    - ◯ pronoun
    - ◯ adjective. What noun does it modify? _____
    - ◯ verb
    - ◯ adverb

23. **smiled**
    - ◯ noun
    - ◯ pronoun
    - ◯ adjective. What noun does it modify? _____
    - ◯ verb
    - ◯ adverb

24. **happily**
    - ◯ noun
    - ◯ pronoun
    - ◯ adjective. What noun does it modify? _____
    - ◯ verb
    - ◯ adverb

25. **mother**
    - ◯ noun
    - ◯ pronoun
    - ◯ adjective. What noun does it modify? _____
    - ◯ verb
    - ◯ adverb

Prepositions

Prepositions are words that link a noun or pronoun to other words in a sentence. Prepositions come in phrases (conveniently called prepositional phrases) that act as one unit. That is important enough to reiterate: prepositional phrases act as a single unit. A prepositional phrase is made up of the preposition, the noun or pronoun that it is relating to (called the object of the preposition), and any adjectives or adverbs that may fall in between the two.

under

> The chair was pushed **under the table**.
>
> ***Under the table*** *is the prepositional phrase.* ***Under*** *is the preposition. Prepositional phrases always start with the preposition.* ***Table*** *is the object of the preposition. Prepositional phrases always end in the noun or pronoun that is the object of the preposition.*

Prepositions show a spatial, time, or logical relationship between the object of the preposition and the rest of the sentence. In the example above, *under the table* shows the chair in terms of space—*where* in space is the chair? Under the table. The most common prepositions are as follows:

aboard	between	past
about	beyond	since
above	but	through
across	by	throughout
after	down	to
against	during	toward
along	except	under
amid	for	underneath
among	from	until
around	in	unto
at	into	up
before	like	upon
behind	of	with
below	off	within
beneath	on	without
beside	over	

So any of these prepositions can be made into prepositional phrases by adding a noun after them and an adjective(s) or adverb(s) between them.

> aboard the boat
> between the pages
> since her last appointment
> from the injury

Now let's see them in action. The following sentences all contain prepositional phrases. Notice the pattern of the prepositional phrases: preposition → adjectives or adverbs (optional) → object of the preposition (noun or pronoun). Also notice how they act as a single unit (like a single part of speech).

The picture **on the wall** was painted **by her grandma**.

The man **with no children** is 63 years old.

After dinner, the couple watched a movie.

He was born **in 1985**.

They walked **to the store in the rain**.

> Note—multiple prepositional phrases often come back to back, like the phrases **to the store** and **in the rain** in this sentence.

Challenge Box

Test yourself on these sentences. Identify the prepositional phrases in the following sentences

1. The house was on the corner.
2. She put a blanket over the window.
3. For the first time, he drove all by himself.
4. They sat on the couch while the children sang to them all.
5. The dog ran down the street.

I. **TRUE/FALSE.**
    If the orange words highlighted are a prepositional phrase, mark True. If they are not, mark False.

1. The lake **was calm** in the morning light.

   ○ true
   ○ false

2. The canoe was tied **by the dock**.

   ○ true
   ○ false

3. As the wind blew, **it rustled** the tree leaves.

   ○ true
   ○ false

4. Birds sang **in the trees**.

   ○ true
   ○ false

5. There was a large cabin **by the water**.

   ○ true
   ○ false

6. They drove the truck **to the cabin** and parked in the clearing.

    ○ true

    ○ false

7. **A squirrel raced** by the tree into the forest.

    ○ true

    ○ false

8. They went hiking **for two hours**.

    ○ true

    ○ false

9. The sun **shone brightly** on the lakeshore.

    ○ true

    ○ false

10. The pine trees smelled **earthy and fresh**.

    ○ true

    ○ false

Conjunctions

Conjunctions are words that join words, phrases, or clauses. The most common type of conjunction is the coordinating conjunction. A **coordinating conjunction** joins two parts of a sentence that are equal in importance. Remember the acronym FANBOY to help recall the coordinating conjunctions: **F**=For, **A**=And, **N**=Nor, **B**=But, **O**=Or, **Y**=Yet.

> The boy ate **and** drank quickly to be on time for football practice.
>
> *The conjunction **and** joins the verbs **ate** and **drank**.* The two words have equal roles in the sentence.
>
> She was told not to run **or** walk too quickly until her ankle healed.
>
> *The conjunction **or** joins the verbs **run** and **walk**.*
>
> He wanted to go to the dance, **but** his parents wouldn't let him.
>
> *The conjunction **but** joins the two independent clauses (sentences).*

Correlative conjunctions are very similar to coordinating conjunctions. **Correlative conjunctions** also join equal parts in a sentence, but correlative conjunctions come in pairs. The common correlative conjunctions are *neither…nor, either…or, both…and, not only…but also,* and *whether…or.*

> **Both** the man **and** his wife were late coming home from work.

> *The correlative conjunctions **both...and** join the nouns **man** and **wife**. Again, these words have equal roles in the sentence.*
>
> **Neither** the newspaper **nor** the Internet made any mention of the incident.
>
> The food **not only** tasted wonderful **but also** was easy to make.

Challenge Box

Test yourself on these sentences. Identify the conjunctions and see if you can determine the type of conjunction.
1. The girl didn't have a dog or a cat.
2. Neither the car nor the truck worked well enough to drive on a long trip.
3. He wanted to hang out with his friend and his girlfriend.

I. PARTS OF SPEECH.
In the following sentences, identify each coordinating conjunction by checking the appropriate box under the words. If a word is NOT a conjunction, do not check the box under that word.

1. The baseball stadium was bright and noisy.

The	baseball	was	bright	and	noisy.
☐	☐	☐	☐	☐	☐

2. The little boy didn't know if he wanted a hot dog or a hamburger.

The	little	boy	didn't	know	if	he	wanted	a	hot	dog	or	a
☐	☐	☐	☐	☐	☐	☐	☐	☐	☐	☐	☐	☐

hamburger.
☐

3. When the player hit the ball, it soared into the stadium.

When	the	player	hit	the	ball,	it	soared	into	the	stadium.
☐	☐	☐	☐	☐	☐	☐	☐	☐	☐	☐

4. The little boy wanted to catch the ball, but he didn't have a baseball mitt.

The	little	boy	wanted	to	catch	the	ball,	but	he	didn't	have	a
☐	☐	☐	☐	☐	☐	☐	☐	☐	☐	☐	☐	☐

baseball	mitt.
☐	☐

5. The announcer cheered, and the crowd yelled in delight.

The	announcer	cheered,	and	the	crowd	yelled	in	delight.
☐	☐	☐	☐	☐	☐	☐	☐	☐

6. The dad bought the little boy a baseball cap.

The	dad	bought	the	little	boy	a	baseball	cap.
☐	☐	☐	☐	☐	☐	☐☐		☐

7. The boy and his father had peanuts and popcorn.

The	boy	and	his	father	had	peanuts	and	popcorn.
☐	☐	☐	☐	☐	☐	☐	☐	☐

8. Everyone was happy when the home team won the game.

Everyone	was	happy	when	the	home	team	won	the	game.
☐	☐	☐	☐	☐	☐	☐	☐	☐	☐

9. It was late when the game finally ended.

It	was	late	when	the	game	finally	ended.
☐	☐	☐	☐	☐	☐	☐	☐

10. The boy didn't want to go home, but the game was over.

The	boy	didn't	want	to	go	home,	but	the	game	was	over.
☐	☐	☐	☐	☐	☐	☐	☐	☐	☐	☐	☐

Unit 3
Sentences

Complete Sentences – Introduction

The sentence is truly the building block of nearly all English writing. (Poetry would be one exception to this rule.) The very definition of a sentence explains why it is so crucial in communicating ideas. Let's begin by looking at what a complete sentence is.

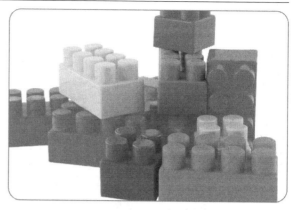

A **sentence:**

- has a subject
- has a predicate
- conveys a complete thought (it can stand by itself)

So, according to the definition, each sentence has a thing or person the sentence is about (the subject). It tells something about the subject (predicate). It contains a complete independent thought and can stand alone. So, each sentence is a neatly encapsulated, autonomous bit of information… Never thought of a sentence that way before? They are powerful tools and ones that you use well every day. Unfortunately, there are quite a few "pretenders" out there that look like sentences but don't meet all of the criteria.

Sentence Fragments

Keep the definition of a sentence in mind—a sentence must have a subject, a predicate, and must convey a complete thought. Problems can occur when any one of the three parts is missing or incomplete:

- If a sentence is missing a subject, it is not a complete sentence.
- If a sentence is missing a predicate, it is not a complete sentence.
- If a sentence does not convey a complete thought while standing alone, it is not a complete sentence.

To be proficient at identifying complete sentences, you should get in the habit of identifying and isolating the **simple subject** and the **simple predicate**. First, isolate the simple predicate, which consists of the main verb (and its helping verbs) in the sentence. Once you have that verb, you can ask yourself, "Who or what is doing that?" Who is running? What is ringing? The answer to that question will be the simple subject—**John** is running. The **phone** is ringing.

So, once you identify the parts of a sentence, you can see if any of these vital parts are missing. If so, the sentence is not really a sentence… it is considered a fragment. A **fragment** is a phrase or clause that is punctuated and capitalized like a sentence but does not have the required parts of a complete sentence.

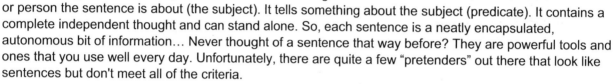

Fragments can be caused by a missing subject:

Wanted a piece of cake.

> *This fragment does not have a subject (the who or what it is about).*

The girl wanted a piece of cake.

> *With the addition of a noun, it is now a complete sentence.*

Fragments can be caused by a missing predicate:

The man with the guitar.

This fragment does not have a predicate (what about the man with the guitar)

The man with the guitar played a song.

With the addition of a verb, the sentence is now complete.

Fragments can be due to an incomplete thought (or a thought that cannot stand alone):

While the boy sat on the porch.

Subject = the boy
Predicate = sat on the porch

*This fragment does not have a complete thought that can stand alone. The conjunction **while** makes this dependent (it would rely on additional information to make the thought complete).*

While the boy sat on the porch, he ate an apple.

It is now a complete sentence.

I. **MULTIPLE CHOICE.**
   For each of the following sentence fragments, mark the reason why the item is a fragment.

   1. The house on the corner.
      ○ missing subject
      ○ missing predicate
      ○ has subject and predicate, but is an incomplete thought

   2. The woman and her boyfriend.
      ○ missing subject
      ○ missing predicate
      ○ has subject and predicate, but is an incomplete thought

   3. After he had eaten.
      ○ missing subject
      ○ missing predicate
      ○ has subject and predicate, but is an incomplete thought

   4. Wanted to go swimming.
      ○ missing subject
      ○ missing predicate
      ○ has subject and predicate, but is an incomplete thought

5. Because she ran too quickly.
   - ○ missing subject
   - ○ missing predicate
   - ○ has subject and predicate, but is an incomplete thought

6. Jumped into the car.
   - ○ missing subject
   - ○ missing predicate
   - ○ has subject and predicate, but is an incomplete thought

7. Sat in front of the fire.
   - ○ missing subject
   - ○ missing predicate
   - ○ has subject and predicate, but is an incomplete thought

8. The bully's father.
   - ○ missing subject
   - ○ missing predicate
   - ○ has subject and predicate, but is an incomplete thought

9. When they walked to the park.
   - ○ missing subject
   - ○ missing predicate
   - ○ has subject and predicate, but is an incomplete thought

10. Followed her to the restaurant.
    - ○ missing subject
    - ○ missing predicate
    - ○ has subject and predicate, but is an incomplete thought

Fixing Fragments

Once you have identified **why** a fragment is a fragment, making it into a complete sentence is usually pretty simple. If you add in the missing element(s), you can generally create a good, complete sentence without having to do much rearrangement.

The young girl with brown hair.

This is missing a predicate. If you add a predicate the sentence becomes complete.

The young girl with brown hair…
…talked to her mother.
…played with her dog.
…ate her lunch.

There are many ways to make fragments into complete sentences. If you have a subject and predicate but the fragment does not express a complete thought that can stand alone, you can make a complete sentence by adding or removing words so that the dependent clause is no longer dependent upon anything.

When the woman and her friend met for dinner.

*This has a subject (patient) and a predicate (arrived), but the word **when** makes this clause dependent. If this word is removed, the clause is now independent (which makes it a sentence).*

The woman and her friend met for dinner.

Or you can add words to connect the dependent clause to an independent clause.

When the woman and her friend met for dinner, they were joined by another friend.

I. MULTIPLE CHOICE.
Choose the item that is a complete sentence.

1. ○ The dinner was ready.
   ○ While the dinner was being made.
   ○ Sat while the dinner was being made.

2. ○ His mother and father.
   ○ He was asked to set the table.
   ○ When he was asked to set the table.

3. ○ Dinner was served after.
   ○ When they had finished.
   ○ Dinner was served when they had finished preparing it.

4. ○ The family ate together.
   ○ Because the family ate together.
   ○ Ate together every night.

5. ○ His father's favorite was the soup.
   ○ His father's favorite.
   ○ Enjoyed the soup.

6. ○ After dinner it was time.
   ○ Time for dessert.
   ○ After dinner it was time for dessert.

7.　　○ His mother had made.
　　　○ His mother had made his favorite dessert.
　　　○ Even though his mother had made his favorite dessert.

8.　　○ After his mother brought it in.
　　　○ He shouted with delight when his mother brought it in.
　　　○ When his mother brought it in.

Run-Ons and Comma Splices

The term *run-on sentence* is a general term that comprises several common sentence structure mistakes. From the definition of a sentence that was presented a couple of pages ago, we can look at why run-on sentences are incorrect, what makes a sentence(s) a run-on, and how to correct run-on sentences.

Remember, a sentence:

- has a subject
- has a predicate
- conveys a complete thought (it can stand by itself)

Most run-on sentences are simply due to a lack of proper punctuation. By definition a **run-on sentence** is two or more sentences (independent clauses) that are connected without any punctuation.

He wanted to get there on time he decided it was time to go.

You have two independent clauses that each could stand alone, but they are connected without any punctuation. This is a run-on sentence.

Run-ons like this can really only be corrected in one of two ways—you can join the two clauses or you can separate the two clauses.

He wanted to get there on time. He decided it was time to go.

Since this run-on is simply two sentences, they could be separated into two sentences.

He wanted to get there on time, so he decided it was time to go.

The two independent clauses can be joined by a coordinating conjunction (and, but, for, or, nor, so, yet) and a comma.

He wanted to get there on time; he decided it was time to go.

If the two clauses are closely related in topic, they can be separated by a semicolon.

> *There is a common thread in all of the corrections made: the run-on, which could not stand alone as a complete thought, can now stand alone as one sentence or two separate sentences.*

If you were going to splice two pieces of the electrical cord on your toaster together, you would not use masking tape. Masking tape is the wrong tool for the job. That splice would cause a health and fire hazard. Similarly, when you go to splice two independent clauses together, you do not use a comma. It, too, is the wrong tool for the job.

Often, comma splices are grouped in with run-on sentences because they basically have the same result—a structure that cannot stand alone. A **comma splice** is a sentence that is created by joining two independent clauses with a comma.

The teacher had 25 students, she loved teaching them all.

> *You have two independent clauses that could each stand alone, but they are connected with a comma. This is a comma splice.*

The teacher had 25 students, and she loved teaching them all.

> *Again, the two independent clauses can be joined by a coordinating conjunction and a comma.*

The teacher had 25 students. She loved teaching them all.

> *The two independent clauses can be separated by a period.*

The most common comma splice you will see is the use of a comma and a conjunctive adverb to join two independent clauses. Some common conjunctive adverbs are *however, also, likewise, therefore, similarly, nonetheless, indeed,* and *consequently.* These **cannot** join two independent clauses, even with the help of a comma! The clauses must be separated by a semicolon or a period.

The college student was hungry, however, she didn't have enough money to buy any lunch.

> *This is incorrect. These independent clauses need to be separated correctly (period or semicolon) or joined correctly (comma and a coordinating conjunction).*

The college student was hungry; however, she didn't have enough money to buy any lunch.

OR

The college student was hungry, but she didn't have enough money to buy any lunch.

I. MULTIPLE CHOICE.
Choose the best answer.

1. The woman was traveling in Europe she had never been there before.
   - ○ run-on
   - ○ comma splice
   - ○ complete sentence

2. She started her trip in England, where her ancestors were from.
   - ○ run-on
   - ○ comma splice
   - ○ complete sentence

3. She visited Shakespeare's birthplace, Stratford-upon-Avon, and then spent time touring London.
   - ○ run-on
   - ○ comma splice
   - ○ complete sentence

4. After touring England, she traveled to France, she didn't speak the language but still enjoyed it.
   - ○ run-on
   - ○ comma splice
   - ○ complete sentence

5. She toured several of the ancient castles, this was after she spent time in the Louvre museum in Paris.
   - ○ run-on
   - ○ comma splice
   - ○ complete sentence

6. Next, she took a train to Italy, where she toured many beautiful cathedrals.
   - ○ run-on
   - ○ comma splice
   - ○ complete sentence

7. After taking a gondola ride in Venice, she ate at a wonderful restaurant they gave her free dessert.
   - ○ run-on
   - ○ comma splice
   - ○ complete sentence

8. Her boyfriend was supposed to meet her back in England his plane was late.
   - ○ run-on
   - ○ comma splice
   - ○ complete sentence

9. When he finally arrived, she was able to show him around some of her favorite places in London.
   - ○ run-on
   - ○ comma splice
   - ○ complete sentence

10. The woman had a wonderful time on her trip, she was ready to go home and share her adventures.
    - ○ run-on
    - ○ comma splice
    - ○ complete sentence

Unit 4
Punctuation

Punctuation – Introduction

If there is one part of the English language that aggravates and torments most people, it would be punctuation. While most language skills seem very artistic, punctuation seems almost mathematical. What is the purpose of punctuation? Believe it or not, it is meant to make dealing with language easier... although that does not always seem to be the case. Punctuation was first formally and consistently used about 600 years ago (when printing began to replace hand copying). To this day, it is used to allow writers to convey their thoughts with precision. Punctuation can be used to remove confusion, signal pauses and stops, create inflection, and add meaning to writing. It allows the reader to absorb the language the way the writer intended. Without the proper punctuation, our language would be even more difficult than it already is.

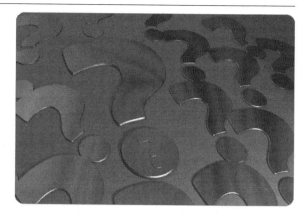

> **Jake picked up cream cheese and sugar from the store.**

According to the punctuation in this sentence, Jake bought two items: cream cheese and sugar. It sounds like Jake is planning on baking something. With the addition of commas, Jake's list changes.

> **Jake picked up cream, cheese, and sugar from the store.**

Jake now has three items that he got from the store: cream, cheese, and sugar. He may still be baking, but his ingredients are certainly different. The presence, absence, or position of punctuation can have significant effects on the meaning of our writing.

In this unit, we will focus on the most important and common pieces of punctuation and their uses.

Commas with Independent Clauses and Series

Commas are the most commonly used—thus, the most commonly incorrectly used—mark of punctuation. Be certain, however, that you understand and can use commas properly. As you study the following uses of commas, be sure that you are comfortable with your understanding of them before continuing.

Commas to join independent clauses

The term **independent clause** is a fancy term for a sentence. A comma and a coordinating conjunction (remember F-A-N-B-O-Y-S) can be used to join two independent clauses.

> The woman called a plumber. He came to fix the sink the next day.
> The woman called a plumber, and he came to fix the sink the next day.
>
> It was late when they started the movie. The girl fell asleep in the middle.
> It was late when they started the movie, so the girl fell asleep in the middle.

Commas to separate items in a series

Use commas to separate three or more items in a series. Remember, the items may be single words, phrases, or clauses.

The boy wanted sprinkles, nuts, and a cherry on his ice cream sundae.

The night was quiet, dark, and cold.

She grabbed her coat, ran out the door, and raced down the stairs.

He didn't like dogs, cats, or birds.

Do not, however, place a comma before the first item in a series, and generally do not place one after the last item in a series.

They bought popcorn, soda, and candy at the movie.

Her cold made her cough, sneeze, and sniffle.

The man was tall, dark, and handsome.

She opened the door, sneaked across the room, and slipped silently into her bedroom.

In all the examples above, a comma appears before the conjunction preceding the final element of the series. This is the classically correct style and has become widely accepted and even considered "the only correct way" by many. However, some styles (such as the AP style) prefer that the last comma be removed.

Do not use commas when multiple words in a series are separated by *and* or *or*.

He didn't want chicken or beef or fish.

She ate vegetables and fruit and bread for lunch.

> *It is quite uncommon to see sentences like this, but you should be aware of how to punctuate them should they come up.*

I. PROOFREADING.
The following sentences may or may not have all required punctuation. Add the necessary commas to make each sentence complete.

1. The girl was very eclectic in her music tastes but she preferred to listen to classical music.

2. Some of her favorite composers were Bach Mozart and Chopin.

3. She enjoyed playing classical music on the piano and she often bought new music to learn.

4. She often went to concerts recitals and performances.

5. Her favorite instruments were the violin and piano and harp.

Commas with Introductions

Commas are used to set off an introductory phrase or clause from the main independent clause.

> Although she didn't usually enjoy watching football, she went to support her son.
>
> **She went to support her son** is the main clause. The introduction precedes it and is set off by a comma.

Usually participial, infinitive, and nonessential phrases that begin a sentence are set off by a comma.

> Thinking he had already bought milk, he didn't go to the grocery store.
>
> To improve his chances of passing the exam, he studied for two weeks.
>
> A fairly long and arduous test, the bar exam was difficult for many law students.

Prepositional phrases used as introductions to a main clause are generally not followed by a comma unless they are long (4 words or longer).

> In the night the cat often hunted mice.
>
> *But*
>
> From the excessive amount of protesting, she became sure her friend actually had feelings for their neighbor.

Sometimes single words alone can be used as introductions. If the words *however, also, no, yes,* or *well* are used as introductory elements, they require a comma after them.

> However, it wasn't as late as he'd thought.
>
> Well, I'll have to reschedule the party.

Challenge Box

Test yourself on these sentences. Where would you put commas in the following sentences or would you not put any at all?

1. After a long and very intense exercise session she felt as if her heart were pounding too hard to be healthy.
2. Since she didn't want to leave her cat home alone she took him on vacation with her.
3. Preparing for her wedding she went to an expensive salon.

Commas with Nonessential Elements

Quite often we add extra information that is not necessary to the basic understanding of the sentence into our speech and writing. We refer to this extra information as a **nonessential element**. It is nonessential because the essence of the sentence is fine without this element being there.

The girl, **a pretty little thing**, had her hair done up in pigtails.

> *The phrase **a pretty little thing** simply adds extra (nonessential) information to the sentence. Without it, the sentence would still be complete and make perfect sense.*

The girl had her hair done up in pigtails.

> *Because the sentence would make sense without the phrase, we can deem it a nonessential element. If they appear in the middle of a sentence, nonessential elements are set aside by using a comma before and after the phrase, clause, or word that is nonessential.*

His workout routine, **both cardio and strength training**, is vigorous.

The man's sister, **who was much younger than him**, decided to set him up with her friend.

We walked down the street to a local restaurant, **an authentic Indian place**.

> *Nonessential elements may also appear at the end of a sentence.*

Essential phrases and clauses **do not** get separated from the main sentence with commas because they are essential to the understanding of the sentence.

The theatre **at the corner of 8th and Center** is where she will be performing.

> *To check and see whether or not this clause is essential or nonessential, take it out of the sentence.*

The theatre is where she will be performing.

> *While the sentence is still a sentence, it is missing some very essential information: which theatre?*

The man's eyeglasses **with the bifocal lenses** give him a headache when he reads.

> *Again, this is essential to the understanding of the sentence.*

The teenager **who hit her with the car** was transported by helicopter to a nearby facility.

> *Again, this is essential to the understanding of the sentence.*

I. MULTIPLE CHOICE.
Choose the sentence with the correct punctuation.

1. ○ For now, he decided not to move out of his apartment.
   ○ For now he decided not to move out of his apartment.

2. ○ Because she hadn't eaten enough that day, she felt weak.
   ○ Because she hadn't eaten enough that day she felt weak.

3. ○ Because he was out of the country he missed his cousin's wedding.
   ○ Because he was out of the country, he missed his cousin's wedding.

4. ○ After she was satisfied with the wrapping, she was ready to give her husband his birthday present.
   ○ After she was satisfied with the wrapping she was ready to give her husband his birthday present.

5. ○ The cars that were new were placed at the front display of the car lot.
   ○ The cars, that were new, were placed at the front display of the car lot.

6. ○ The dog a six-year-old cocker spaniel bounded up to its owner in excitement.
   ○ The dog, a six-year-old cocker spaniel, bounded up to its owner in excitement.

7. ○ The child was found to be happy not to mention healthy when he spent more of his time running around outside.
   ○ The child was found to be happy, not to mention healthy, when he spent more of his time running around outside.

8. ○ A friendly and confident person, she was a good choice for the prom queen.
   ○ A friendly and confident person she was a good choice for the prom queen.

9. ○ The man had a bookshelf, with no books in it.
   ○ The man had a bookshelf with no books in it.

10. ○ Between you and me I don't think I would have worn pants to a party like this.
    ○ Between you and me, I don't think I would have worn pants to a party like this.

Commas with Coordinate Adjectives and Parenthetical Elements

Commas With Coordinate Adjectives

Often, people will use two or more adjectives of equal importance in a row to describe something. These adjectives are called **coordinate adjectives**.

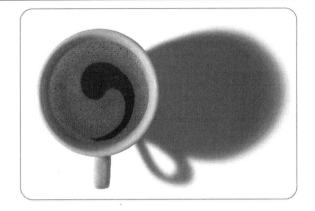

> The paper had a **jagged, torn** edge.
>
> *The adjectives **jagged** and **torn** are of equal importance. They should be separated by a comma.*

Not all adjectives positioned next to each other are coordinate adjectives (and, therefore, do not require a comma to separate them). Some adjectives have different degrees of importance in relation to the noun or pronoun they are modifying. To tell whether adjectives are coordinate, you can ask yourself two questions. If the answer to both of these is *yes*, then you have coordinate adjectives and must put a comma between them.

1. Could you put the word ***and*** between the two adjectives and still have the sentence make sense?
2. Could you change the order of the adjectives and still have the sentence make sense?

> She is an independent, active female.
>
> *Question #1- Could you put the word **and** between the two adjectives and still have the sentence make sense?*
> *Answer- Yes. She is an independent and active female.*
>
> *Question #2- Could you change the order of the adjectives and still have the sentence make sense?*
> *Answer- Yes. She is an active, independent female.*
>
> *Since we answered yes to these, we see they are of equal importance and our comma belongs between them.*
>
> He broke his right middle toe.
>
> *Question #1- Could you put the word **and** between the two adjectives and still have the sentence make sense?*
> *Answer- No. He broke his right and middle toe.*
>
> *Since we answered **no** to the first question, we don't need to go any further. These are not coordinate adjectives and don't require a comma.*

Commas With Parenthetical Elements

There are certain words we often use in sentences to add emphasis, order, or personal thoughts to the sentence. These are known as **parenthetical elements** (because they could be put in parentheses as well). When a parenthetical element is used in a sentence, it is set off with commas.

Her mother, to be honest with you, isn't quite as friendly as she is.

The guitar, however, must be tuned first.

I called him today, as I mentioned earlier, to discuss the upcoming event.

Troublesome Comma Rules

Common Misuse of Commas With Dependent Clauses

One of the first rules of comma use you learn when you are in elementary school is the use of a comma and a coordinating conjunction (*for, and, nor, but, or, yet*) to join two independent clauses (sentences). This rule, however, often gets applied in situations where it should not be applied and creates a misuse of the comma.

Do not join an independent and a dependent clause or phrase with a comma and a conjunction the way you would two independent clauses.

Correct: She took her sister by the hand, and they ran across the beach.

There is an independent clause on each side of the comma so they can be joined with the comma and the conjunction "and".

Incorrect: He arrived late, and appeared to be upset.

"Appeared to be upset" is a phrase and cannot be joined to an independent clause with a comma and conjunction. The conjunction by itself will suffice.

Correct: He arrived late and appeared to be upset.

Common Misuse of Commas With Conjunctive Adverbs

Another common misuse of the comma is using the comma and certain transitional words (mainly conjunctive adverbs) to join two sentences. Some common conjunctive adverbs are: *also, however, likewise, nonetheless, therefore, similarly, consequently, so, otherwise*.

These words are not real conjunctions even though they are transition words. They can join two independent clauses; they just require different punctuation.

Correct: The man knew the risks of skydiving, but he decided to do it anyway.

In this sentence, two independent clauses were joined by a comma plus the coordinating conjunction "but".

Incorrect: The man knew the risks of skydiving, however he opted to do it anyway.

Conjunctive adverbs (unlike coordinating conjunctions) cannot be used with a comma to join two independent clauses. They require a semicolon (before) and a comma (after).

Correct: The man knew the risks of skydiving; however, he opted to do it anyway.

Or

The man knew the risks of skydiving. However, he opted to do it anyway.

Note: *The conjunctive adverbs "so" and "therefore" do not always require a comma to follow them when used in this way. This is one of the wonderful, mysterious rules of our language that makes it challenging to master.*

Correct: The man knew the risks of skydiving; so he opted to do it anyway.

I. MULTIPLE CHOICE.
Choose the sentence that has the correct use of commas.

1. ○ The boat was prepped for a long, enjoyable ride.
   ○ The boat was prepped for a long enjoyable ride.

2. ○ The four friends climbed aboard and sat down.
   ○ The four friends climbed aboard, and sat down.

3. ○ They were ready to go, however, the boat needed extra gas.
   ○ They were ready to go; however, the boat needed extra gas.

4. ○ Finally, the boat took off into the water and the friends began to laugh.
   ○ Finally, the boat took off into the water, and the friends began to laugh.

5. ○ The boat was fast, and the cool, refreshing wind blew through their hair.
   ○ The boat was fast, and the cool refreshing wind blew through their hair.

Periods

Periods are used at the end of a statement or complete sentence. When typing, periods (and all end marks, such as question marks and exclamation points) are usually followed by one space. In years past, two spaces was a common standard. In practical application, you will most likely be allowed to use either one or two spaces following end marks. However, be aware that you may be required to conform to the preferences of a professional style guide.

A misplaced period can cause you to have strings of several run-on sentences in your writing. Conversely, arbitrarily throwing them in where they do not belong creates incomplete sentences or sentence fragments. Both of these errors make your writing appear sloppy and can cause a reader to misunderstand the intended meaning of the sentence.

The following is a reiteration of some common rules involving periods. This should be second nature to you.

Rule 1: *Primarily, periods are used to separate sentences.*

The improper use of a period to separate a sentence can create a sentence fragment. Likewise, failure to use a period where necessary leads to a run-on sentence.

Rule 2: *Periods are used in names and titles, such as Mr. and Mrs. or Dr.*

In this case, the period is always followed by only one space on your keyboard.

I. PROOFREADING.
   Proofread the following sentences. Add periods wherever they are missing.

1. Dr Johnson wanted to take a vacation He called Mrs Johnson to tell her they were going to Maine

2. When he came home, his wife was thrilled They scheduled the trip and packed

3. The flight was not long and then they arrived They traveled to their bed and breakfast

4. They enjoyed a meal of delicious clam chowder That evening they walked along a beautiful beach

5. After their trip was over they were ready to go home They were happy to have had such a great vacation

Colons

The colon is a piece of punctuation that has a more specific and focused purpose than many others. The colon is used to connect an independent clause to a list, explanation, rule, or quotation. The colon creates a harder "stop" than the comma or semicolon, and it does not have the variety of uses that some other punctuation has.

At this point, we will assume you know the basic uses of the colon. If you are not comfortable with the following uses of the colon, now is a great time to review them. There are many free grammar resources on the Web. The rules you need to be familiar with that we will not review are as follows:

- Insert a colon after a greeting in a business letter (Dear Mr. Chambers:)
- Insert a colon in expressions of time (3:32 A.M.)

Use a colon to connect an independent clause to a list.

> The man had the following favorite types of food: Mexican, Italian, and Greek.
>
> *The independent clause contains the phrase "the following", which is a signal that a colon and a list will come next. As a reader, you can generally anticipate what will follow a colon.*

Use a colon to connect an independent clause to an explanation or rule.

> The doctor gave him the following instructions: do not work out with free weights for at least six weeks and ice the elbow liberally.
>
> *It is generally acceptable not to capitalize a sentence that comes after the colon (like in this example). If you have a situation where two or more sentences follow the colon, then you would*

capitalize each one. Of course, if a proper noun follows the colon, the proper noun will begin with a capital letter.

The exception to this is when a rule follows the colon. If you have a rule that follows a colon, begin that rule with a capital letter.

There is one rule to losing weight: Always know what your caloric intake is.

Do not use a colon if the clause that introduces the list or rule is not an independent clause (if it could not stand alone).

Incorrect: The man ordered: a burger, fries, and a soda.

Because the introduction "The man ordered" is not an independent clause (cannot stand alone), a colon should not be used here. In this case the list can be incorporated into one single sentence.

Correct: The man ordered a burger, fries, and a soda.

I. **MULTIPLE CHOICE.**
Choose the sentence with the correct punctuation.

1. ○ He wanted two things: a puppy and a wagon.
   ○ He wanted two things, a puppy and a wagon.

2. ○ After the accident the man had the following, blurred vision, headache, and a sore neck.
   ○ After the accident the man had the following: blurred vision, headache, and a sore neck.

3. ○ The doctor gave her his number one rule concerning prenatal care: You are no longer the most important person in your own life.
   ○ The doctor gave her his number one rule concerning prenatal care, you are no longer the most important person in your own life.

4. ○ The woman had a special name for her two-year-old niece, The Tornado.
   ○ The woman had a special name for her two-year-old niece: The Tornado.

5. ○ She has had: no candy bars, peppermints, or other types of candy for days.
   ○ She has had no candy bars, peppermints, or other types of candy for days.

Parentheses

Parentheses are common in the English language. They set aside parenthetical ideas—those ideas that are not necessary to understanding the sentence. But as we learned earlier, commas can also set aside parenthetical ideas, and as you will learn later, dashes can set aside parenthetical ideas.

So how do you know when to use one and not the other? In general, parentheses denote an aside rather than an addition to existing information.

The man's dog (as he told his friend) was a loyal animal.

She has been taking a lot of medicine (it is Advil, I think) to keep her headaches under control.

Parentheses do not require separate punctuation of their own, but standard punctuation and capitalization rules apply both inside and outside of the parentheses.

He wanted to go to Disneyland. (His parents explained they couldn't go until next year.)

In this case, the sentence inside the parentheses is a complete sentence of its own, so it is capitalized and punctuated like any other complete sentence.

When using parentheses, if you have a parenthetical idea *within* a parenthetical idea, you would use brackets inside of parentheses.

When he was in a car wreck, he was already in a cast (for a completely unrelated reason [he had broken his leg skiing]) and couldn't walk well.

I. **PROOFREADING.**
   Proofread the following sentence.

   1. Her favorite thing to do in her spare time was to ride motorcycles (On a dirt race track, I believe.) She traveled around the country riding her motorcycle [with a team of other racers.]

   2. The man started having problems with his balance eight years ago (It started after a concussion.) He got tired and lost his balance often when he exercised. (he had been running for years)

Hyphens – Lesson 1

One strange little mark that causes a lot of trouble in the English language is the hyphen. A hyphen, unlike a dash, is not a punctuation mark. It is a spelling mark. This distinction can help us understand a little more about its use.

The most common use of hyphens is to create compound modifiers. A compound modifier is created when two words act as a single modifier (adjective) for a noun. Unlike coordinate adjectives, which we learned create a series of modifiers, compound modifiers act as a single unit.

> She had difficulty overcoming her **self-inflicted** guilt.
>
> *In this sentence **self-inflicted** acts as one modifier in its description of the word **guilt**.*
>
> Her **4-year-old** son was much taller than the other children in his class.

You will notice that in all of the previous examples, the compound modifier comes directly before the noun it modifies. Changing the placement of the compound modifier and/or the word it modifies can also change the rules of hyphenation.

Words and numerals are often combined to make compound modifiers.

> 2-liter bottle
> three-piece suit
> 3-dollar fee
>
> *If the compound modifier contains a measurement, it is hyphenated **only if an English unit of measurement is used**; it is not hyphenated if a metric unit abbreviation is used.*
>
> 2-ton load
> 6-pound infant
> 4 mm incision
> 25 mg capsule
> a one-third piece
>
> *Fractions are only hyphenated when they are used as adjectives. If they are used in other ways (like one third of a dose) they are not hyphenated.*

If you switch the order of the noun and the modifiers, the role of the modifiers may change.

> The 21-year-old woman denies any history of alcohol abuse.
>
> *But*
>
> The woman is 21 years old, and she denies any history of alcohol abuse.
>
> *In this sentence, the modifier changed to a simple predicate adjective. It no longer acts as one unit describing the noun, so it is no longer hyphenated. **Usually, if the descriptors are not placed before the word they describe, they will not be hyphenated**.*
>
> Josh is a full-time student.
>
> *But*
>
> Josh goes to school full time.
>
> *Again, the movement of the modifiers to after the noun causes the hyphen to be dropped.*

Unfortunately, you must be very aware of the parts of your compound modifiers to ensure that you use hyphens correctly. If the word *very* or an adverb that ends in *–ly* is part of your compound modifier, you do not use a hyphen. The reason for this is the word *very* or the *–ly* adverb already signals to the reader that this is a compound modifier.

> He claims to have a highly developed sense of smell.
>
> Lorena seems to have very limited desire to attend sporting events.

You do not use a hyphen if your compound modifier is preceded by an adverb.

> The well-developed plot is my favorite part of the book.
>
> *But*
>
> The very well developed plot is my favorite part of the book.
>
> This new-found activity made her happy.
>
> *But*
>
> This seemingly new found activity made her happy.

Hyphens – Lesson 2

Hyphens are used when a prefix is added to a proper noun or a proper adjective. Likewise, words with the prefix *ex-*, *self-*, *all-*, or those with the suffix *–elect* are hyphenated.

> ex-wife
> all-encompassing
> president-elect
> self-aggrandizing
> neo-classical

Remember, numbers 21 through 99 are hyphenated when they are spelled out.

> Thirty-six
> Eighty-nine
> Three hundred forty-five
>
> **Note:** *numbers 21 through 99 may be part of larger numbers, like 246.*

Suspensive hyphenations are those that have two or more hyphenated words in which the second part of the modifier is used only once. These are essentially used to save space in writing.

> Becky cut the fabric into 3-, 6-, and 9-inch pieces.

> *The hyphen is included in all the modifiers, even when they are not complete.*

She has a 5- and a 6-year-old child at home.

While this last rule is a combination and reiteration of earlier rules, it is being presented separately. There are several terms that, depending upon how they are used, may or may not be hyphenated.

The terms followup/follow-up/follow up are commonly used in many fields of work. When it is being used as a compound modifier, it will be hyphenated. It has also become acceptable to write the compound modifier as one word. When it is used as a noun, the term is generally written as one word.

> We scheduled a follow-up appointment for Tuesday.
>
> *OR*
>
> We scheduled a followup appointment for Tuesday.
>
> *Follow-up/followup is being used as a single modifier describing the appointment.*
>
> We scheduled a followup for the next day.
>
> *In this case followup is being used as a noun.*

If the term is being used as a verb (it is something a person is to do), it is presented as two words.

> The client is to follow up with us in one week.
>
> She will follow up with her dentist.

This same principle can be applied to many other terms.

> Her temper will **flare up** at a moment's notice. *(verb)*
>
> There was a **flareup** at the site of the infection. *(noun)*
>
> She used the treadmill to **build up** her stamina. *(verb)*
>
> A **buildup** of plaque resulted in a cavity. *(noun)*

I. PROOFREADING.
Proofread the following sentences.

1. She called her exhusband to see if he was coming to pick up their 9 year old son.

2. He went in for a followup and discussed the xray with his doctor.

3. The president elect gave an inspiring speech.

4. She has a 3, 5, and 9 year old child at home.

Apostrophes – Lesson 1

Most of us learned the rules concerning apostrophes when we were in elementary and middle school. And while the rules remain the same, actuallty applying them adds a new level of complexity to these rules.

We will begin by reviewing the simple rules and then working through some of the exceptions and more difficult rules.

To make a singular noun possessive, simply add an apostrophe + s.

> The girl's sister
>
> The dog's ball
>
> A ruler's length
>
> The teacher's student

Most words that are singular that also end in the letter *s* (or the *s* sound) still follow the original rule: just add an apostrophe + s. In all of these cases, an additional *s* sound is created by the addition to the word. You can hear the additional syllable when you say these words aloud with the extra *s* at the end.

> The boss's report
>
> Chris's parents
>
> The dose's effects
>
> Robert Wise's movies

There are a few words that end in an *s* sound that would sound awkward if an additional *s* sound were added. In this case, simply add an apostrophe. These are rare exceptions.

> Ulysses' adventure
>
> Dr. Moses' charity work

For some reason, there is some confusion surrounding making plural words possessive. There need not be any confusion. To make plural nouns possessive, you only have two choices:

1. If the possessive word ends in the letter *s*, simply add an apostrophe.
2. If the plural word does not end in the letter s, then you resort to the original possessive rule (add apostrophe + s).

The dancers' range of motion

The researchers' conclusions

The children's section

The geese's pen

The women's meeting

Challenge Box

Test yourself on these sentences. How would you punctuate the possessive words in the following sentences?
1. Emma held the purses handle in one hand.
2. He reportedly fainted in the teachers lounge.

Apostrophes – Lesson 2

If you have a business or an organization or a hyphenated word, you make only the last word possessive. If you have two nouns or pronouns that own a thing together, you only make the second noun or pronoun possessive.

The brother-in-law's tests

Hutchings Museum's history

The Agency for International Development's newest proposal

Jack and Carrie's dogs (Jack and Carrie both own the dogs)

Jack's and Carrie's dogs (Jack and Carrie each own a dog)

Units of time, measurement, or currency used as possessives follow the same rules that other possessive words follow.

A week's wait

Two hours' notice

A month's pay

A meter's width

A dollar's worth

Acronyms also follow the same rules that other possessive words follow.

The NFL's top running back

ABC's newest anchor

The DOD's latest report

The CPAs' ledgers (in this case, there is more than one CPA owning ledgers)

The DMDs' preferences (again, in this case DMD is plural and possessive)

When using lower case letters, if you want to make them plural, you can use an apostrophe to keep the reader from being confused. If you use capital letters or numbers, you do not need to use apostrophes.

She often confused f's for e's when reading.

The apostrophe minimizes confusion.

In the 1970s, this test required a lot of preparation.

We compared the CBCs and could tell there had been a remarkable change.

In these examples, there is no need to use an apostrophe.

Some pronouns are possessive by nature. These are called **possessive pronouns**. The possessive pronouns are *mine, yours, his, hers, ours, theirs, whose, my, your, its, their, her*. Since these show ownership in their regular form, you **do not** use apostrophes with them. Do not confuse these with all other pronouns that require apostrophes.

That is her car. — The car is hers.

That is his box. — The box is his.

But

That candy belongs to someone. — That is someone's candy.

The room belongs to nobody. — It is nobody's room.

When you see a prepositional phrase that begins with the word *of* and contains a possessive noun or pronoun, you should always consider revising the sentence for clarity.

Original: He went on a blind date with a friend of his sister's roommate.

The phrasing is awkward and may complicate the idea. This could be revised for clarity.

Revised: He went on a blind date with the roommate of a friend of his sister.

Original: He was in contact with one of her children's chaperone.

Revised: He was in contact with a chaperone of one of her children.

I. MULTIPLE CHOICE.
Choose the best answer.

1. Caeden searched for the (◯mens', ◯men's) room.

2. No (◯ones, ◯one's) results will be returned before next week.

3. She called Mrs. (◯Ross's, ◯Rosses) phone number to ask her a question.

4. After four (◯day's, ◯days') wait, she finally decided to find answers on her own.

5. His (◯father-in-law's, ◯father's-in-law) business was doing very well.

6. The (◯students', ◯students) conclusions were very similar to one another.

7. His (◯mother and father's, ◯mothers' and father's) lecture made him sulk.

8. The mother asked for her (◯childrens', ◯children's) school records.

9. When the dog yanked on (◯it's, ◯its) collar, it pulled the boy down on his knee.

10. Her (◯brother's, ◯brothers') girlfriend came to visit for the holidays.

Quotation Marks

Using quotation marks is important If you are recording information verbatim. In order to be as accurate as possible, you need to know the rules governing punctuation with quotation marks.

Rule 1: *A direct quotation that is a complete sentence always begins with a capital letter. A direct quotation is followed or preceded by an introduction or identifier so the reader knows who is speaking. You will usually see introductions or identifiers like **She said, He announced, I answered, Mary cried, John declared.***

> Mary asked, "When are you leaving for the airport?"
>
> John said, "Give me all your kings."
>
> Harry answered, "Go fish."
>
> "We want some ice cream!" Allyson and Ellie cried.

Rule 2: *Periods and commas are always placed inside quotation marks. There are no exceptions.*

He said he had "the jitters," but they had gone away.

"I feel like my legs are going to fall off."

She described her husband as "the most wonderful man in the world."

Some of the direct quotations in the above examples are not complete sentences. That is why they are not capitalized.

Rule 3: *On the other hand, however, semicolons and colons are always placed outside the quotation marks.*

The following are described as "constant problems": laundry that isn't done, dirty dishes in the sink, and a floor that is never swept.

My grandma complained of "feeling weak"; she also said she was dizzy.

Rule 4: *Finally, question marks and exclamation points are placed inside the closing quotation marks if the* quotation *is an exclamation or question; otherwise, they are placed outside the closing quotation mark.*

"Do you really think I should go?" she kept asking.

At the parent-teacher conference, did Mrs. Kramasz talk to Mark's parents about the "problem areas"?

I. **PROOFREADING.**
    The following sentences are completely without punctuation. Add all commas, periods, quotation marks, etc. as necessary.

    1. She described the issue as a confusion with the delivery of my fees

    2. Stop Stop You can't take my purse she screamed at the thief

    3. He described the color of the skin as sea green

    4. When asked about the headache she said this is the worst pain I have ever felt

    5. The boy repeatedly asked when are we leaving

Unit 5
Capitalization

Capitalization – Introduction

Capitalization is another way in which a writer can signal the reader. Only with capitalization, the signals are different—this is the beginning of a sentence, this is a person's title, this word is important, this is an actual name of a specific group, etc.

You have to know the rules of capitalization in order to apply them. It takes a firm understanding of the conventions of capitalization to create accurate sentences and good writing. To make things easier, we have broken the rules down and will present a few on each page. You will be able to test your knowledge before moving on to the next set of rules.

Capitalization Rules 1–5

Rule 1: Always begin a sentence with a capital letter. This acts as a signal to your reader that this is a new thought.

> The two boys played video games together all afternoon.
>
> There was a rainbow in the sky as the clouds cleared.

Rule 2: Even though we just covered this rule, it is worth reiterating. When using a direct quote, capitalize the first letter of the quote if the quotation is a complete sentence itself. *If it is not a complete sentence, do not capitalize the first letter of the quotation.*

> Her aunt gave her a hug and said, "It's nice to see you again."
>
> She told me the pain is "like someone pinching me."

Rule 3: Capitalize the first letter after a colon if there are two or more sentences *in the statement following the colon. If there is one sentence, phrase, or clause after the colon, it does not get capitalized.*

> He had to do two things before leaving the country: First, he had to get a passport. Second, he needed a visa.
>
> I believe we have a single objective here: to find the driver of the totalled car.

Rule 4: If the introductory portion of the sentence (prior to the colon) is very short and the heart of the material comes after the colon, capitalize the sentence coming after the colon. If the introduction and colon are used to introduce a rule, capitalize the first letter after the colon.

Always remember this: The best cookies have chocolate, nuts, and oatmeal.

I told her the first rule of recovery: Remove from your life that which initially caused the injury.

Rule 5: *If you have a list that is separated into outline form (lettering or numbering the items), the beginning of each item in the list is capitalized, whether they are complete sentences or not.*

Requirements:
1. Have a driver's license
2. Be CPR certified
3. Obtain a food handler's permit

I. **PROOFREADING.**
   Proofread the following sentences. Insert punctuation as required.

   1. keep this in mind: the only way in is through the front door.

   2. The little girl is Right Handed. she has not had many blood draws in the left arm.

   3. His health required the following rigorous diet: increased fiber, decreased dairy, and no sodas at all.

   4. It was late when she arrived home. the clock in her bedroom read 2:03.

   5. she had to buy the following ingredients at the store: milk, bread, and eggs.

Capitalization Rules 6–10

Rule 6: *Titles of people get capitalized if they are being used as part of or in place of a person's name. If the title is merely being used as a description, do not capitalize it.*

She has worked for Congressman Aldridge for four years.

He was brought here today by Pastor Allamance, his church pastor.

He thought for a long time and said, "I think I can do this, Coach."

But

I spoke with his pastor about possible counseling.

We will ask his mother to come in.

Rule 7: *Capitalize a person's credentials when they follow the person's name, whether they are spelled out or abbreviated. Do not capitalize the credentials if they are just being used as a general reference rather than part of a person's title.*

She was referred to us by Albert Pas, MD.

We referred her to Steven Showalter, Doctor of Dental Surgery.

But

She was considering studying to be a doctor of dental surgery.

Rule 8: *The full names of companies, organizations, associations, government entities, foundations, and clubs are capitalized.*

She claimed to have researched the illness through the National Institute of Health.

When Sears closed down, she lost her job.

The Department of Labor did not have good news for her.

Tip: The word **the** *does not get capitalized unless it is part of the title (or unless it begins the sentence, as it does in this case).*

Rule 9: *In some specialty areas, like medical reports, both department and clinic names are used. This can cause some confusion, so we'll break it down into two parts to make it clear.*

Common department names that are being used as references to a general department are not capitalized. If the proper name of the department/clinic is used, the name is capitalized.

She was told that the wait at the emergency room was going to be several hours; so she went back home.

She came to us from Central Coast Pain Clinic.

We released the patient on the grounds that he would follow up at the hearing clinic.

She was told that she would have to go to Cove City Hearing Specialties for her tests.

Rule 10: *This is another rule that applies in medical areas, but it can cross over into other fields as well. You will often see cases when writers refer to a specialty as an entity in and of itself, encompassing the building, the people, and the department all in one. For instance, "We will send the patient to Oncology." In this case, the reference is to the oncology department without saying so. When a department name is used in this fashion, it is capitalized. You should see a difference between this use (representing the department) and the common use of the specialty term.*

We referred her to Hematology and will follow up after her appointment.

*In this sentence, **Hematology** is used to represent the building, the people, and the department.*

When the patient arrived, she brought her hematology report from her visit last spring.

*In this sentence, **hematology** is just the specialty.*

We are awaiting results from Pathology.

The pathology results will be back on Tuesday.

Challenge Box

Test yourself. What letters in the following sentences should be capitalized?
1. Once we get the results from doctor Bateman, we may refer her to a pain clinic.
2. This patient suffered an injury to her femur during her work in the us postal service.
3. This patient will be seen by cardiology immediately, and I will consult with Jared Decker, md, facc.
4. If we get the pulmonary tests back, we will have her follow up with east wayne pulmonary center.

I. MULTIPLE CHOICE.
Choose the sentence with the correct use of capitalization.

1. the consulting doctor ordered the patient to radiology for an immediate x-ray.

   ○ The consulting Doctor ordered the patient to Radiology for an immediate X-ray.
   ○ The consulting doctor ordered the patient to Radiology for an immediate x-ray.
   ○ The consulting doctor ordered the patient to radiology for an immediate x-ray.

2. at this time we will ask the patient to follow up with dr. alec at the podiatry clinic.

   ○ At this time we will ask the patient to follow up with Dr. Alec at the Podiatry Clinic.
   ○ At this time we will ask the patient to follow up with dr. Alec at the podiatry clinic.
   ○ At this time we will ask the patient to follow up with Dr. Alec at the podiatry clinic.

3. he stopped by the national broadcasting company's headquarters when he toured the city.

   ○ He stopped by The National Broadcasting company's headquarters when he toured the City.
   ○ he stopped by the National Broadcasting Company's Headquarters when he toured the city.
   ○ He stopped by the National Broadcasting Company's headquarters when he toured the city.

4. she was escorted to early dawn mental health clinic by officer mason.

   ○ She was escorted to us from Early Dawn mental health by officer Mason.

   ○ She was escorted to us from early dawn mental health by Officer Mason.

   ○ She was escorted to us from Early Dawn Mental Health by Officer Mason.

5. he filled out a worker's compensation claim when he was injured while working for the city.

   ○ he filled out a worker's compensation claim when he was injured while working for the City.

   ○ He filled out a worker's compensation claim when he was injured while working for the city.

   ○ He filled out a worker's compensation claim when he was injured while working for The City.

Capitalization Rules 11–14

Rule 11: *Days of the week, months of the year, holidays, and religious observances are capitalized. Seasons of the year are* not *capitalized.*

We will see her back on the first Monday in June.

She had a severe bout of depression when she was home for Christmas.

She said she changed her diet drastically during Lent.

The patient was seen in this clinic last spring.

Rule 12: *Directions on a compass do not get capitalized when they are referring to cardinal directions. However, if the direction is being used as a place (the South, the Midwest), then it should be capitalized.*

She arrived in the Northeast with her family for a vacation.

The dry air of the West helped his allergies tremendously.

The school is 20 miles northeast of here.

She was headed south on the interstate when she got in an accident.

Rule 13: *Most acronyms and initialisms are capitalized. However, there are some that have become common nouns through usage (scuba, radar). The words that the acronym comes from are not capitalized unless they are proper nouns.*

She was rushed to the CICU upon arrival.

but

She was rushed to the cardiac intensive care unit upon arrival.

The technique was recently approved by the ARA.

The technique was recently approved by the Academy of Rehabilitative Audiology.

In this case, the words that create the acronym also stand as a proper noun in their expanded form.

Rule 14: *Races, nationalities, religions, and tribes are capitalized. The exception to this rule is when the words* white *or* black *are used to describe a person's race. If a person's race is designated* white *or* black*, the word is* not *capitalized.*

The candidate is an elderly Caucasian man, an established resident.

The adoption papers for the girl described her as a 12-year-old African American female.

She described the robber as a white male, about six feet tall.

Challenge Box

Test yourself. What letters in the following sentences should be capitalized?
1. Tick-borne diseases like this are not uncommon in the north this time of year.
2. The patient has been exposed to severe acute respiratory syndrome, also known as sars.
3. She is a hispanic woman from a town east of columbia, south carolina.
4. If her progress continues, we will see her in july and then not again until fall.

I. **TRUE/FALSE.**
   The capitalization in the following sentences is correct: true or false?

   1. The child was transferred to the nicu on Monday, January 4.

      ◯ true
      ◯ false

   2. She claimed they moved here from the Midwest last fall.

      ◯ true
      ◯ false

   3. She often babysat her neighbor, a two-year-old hispanic boy.

      ◯ true
      ◯ false

4. The girl injured herself during a relay race on Easter morning.

     ◯ true
     ◯ false

5. Since last May, she has been treated for GERD (Gastroesophageal Reflux Disease).

     ◯ true
     ◯ false

Unit 6
Agreement

Agreement – Introduction

Have you ever wandered through a neighborhood and seen a house that just didn't fit in? You are not sure if it's the architecture or the building material—maybe it's the color or the landscaping. From the time we are young, we are trained to notice things that are different. We seem to work more comfortably and efficiently in patterns.

It makes sense, then, that our language is one of patterns. As we piece the words together to make sentences and the sentences together to make paragraphs, the patterns must remain the same. If something within a sentence breaks the pattern the writer set forth, it stands out to the reader like a brick Victorian in a neighborhood of pastel beach bungalows. When a sentence or paragraph has a structure in which all things follow the same pattern, it is said to be in agreement. The term *agreement* can refer to many things within a piece of writing:

- verb tense agreement
- subject/verb agreement
- pronoun agreement

In addition to these types of agreement, there are several elements of language that help ensure the patterns within a sentence or paragraph remain fluid and consistent:

- pronoun case
- pronoun reference
- modifier placement
- parallel structure

A piece of writing that is in agreement flows harmoniously and without hesitation. That's the kind of writing you should strive for all the time! Sounds a little daunting, right? Don't worry. The more you practice, the easier it will be.

Tense Agreement

When you were in middle school and high school and you were working through your English and composition classes, you were probably reminded to "Keep your verb tense consistent" by way of bright red marks in the margins of your essays. Whatever you are writing now, you will usually utilize one main verb tense. This verb tense—past, present, or any other tense—is used as a reference for the time of other events in the writing. In other words, you may be writing in the present tense, but you can use the past tense in the same writing to signal to the reader that this event took place prior to the rest of the information. So, maintaining consistent verb tense does not mean using the same verb tense all throughout your writing. It does mean, however, that you must keep all references to a particular time in one tense, while using other appropriate tenses to signal changes in time within the text.

Her dog, Buddy, **was** sick yesterday, but he **is** fine now.

*The verb **was** is in the past tense, letting us know that at some point prior to the present (with the present representing the time of dictation), the subject's dog was sick.*

*The verb **is** is in the present tense and lets us know that at this point, the dog is fine.*

> *Even though there are two different verb tenses in one sentence, there is consistency because the two do not conflict with one another.*

Verb tense agreement problems occur when the writer uses different verb tenses when referring to the same time or when conflicting verb tenses create ambiguity.

> When his cast was removed at the end of the summer, Blake tells his mother that his arm still hurts.
>
> *There is certainly some problem with verb agreement in this sentence. The verb phrase **was removed** is in the past tense, but the second verb, **tells**, is in the present tense. This creates confusion about when the two events happened in relation to one another.*
>
> When his cast was removed at the end of the summer, Blake told his mother that his arm still hurt.
>
> *By putting both verbs in the past tense, the reader now understands that both the removal and the complaints of pain occurred in the past.*

Sometimes the agreement problem, like the one in the example above, stands out and the reader's confusion is the first signal that there is a problem. Sometimes, however, the differences are subtle and a keen editing eye is needed to catch them.

> The pain in the arm radiates to the elbow and moved down from the shoulder.
>
> *The verb **radiates** (present tense) indicates that this is happening in the present. The verb **moved** is in the past tense. If the pain moved from the shoulder at some point in the past and ceased moving, then this could be correct. If the pain continues to move down from the shoulder as it radiates to the elbow, then **moved** should be changed to **moves**.*
>
> *Your understanding of the context, based on what is said or written before and after the sentence will help you make the right determination.*

I. **TRUE/FALSE.**
   The verb tenses in the following sentences are in agreement: true or false?

   1. Since his birthday was on Thursday, his parents decide to throw him a surprise party.

      ○ true
      ○ false

   2. His mom baked a cake and his dad called his friends to let them know about the party.

      ○ true
      ○ false

   3. They decided to hold the party in their basement, so they start to decorate it.

      ○ true
      ○ false

4. They use lots of streamers, and they had to go to the store twice to get enough.

   ○ true
   ○ false

5. The cake was chocolate, which was their son's favorite flavor.

   ○ true
   ○ false

6. They bought several presents for him, including some books he had told them he wanted.

   ○ true
   ○ false

7. The father took his son out that night and all of his friends arrive for the party while he is gone.

   ○ true
   ○ false

8. Everyone hid when they heard the father and son drive up outside.

   ○ true
   ○ false

9. When he walked in the front door, everyone jumps out and yells happy birthday.

   ○ true
   ○ false

10. The boy laughed and thanks all his friends for coming.

   ○ true
   ○ false

Subject/Verb Agreement

As children, we pick up on the subtleties of language through imitation and trial and error. You may hear a young child say, "You swims good." It is cute when a kid says it. It is not cute when an adult says it...or worse yet, writes or types it. Children will make mistakes when they try to create impromptu sentences because they are quickly (without thought) putting subjects and predicates together. They have not yet learned that certain subjects require certain verbs so that the two will agree in number.

Since we will be using the terms *subject* and *predicate* over and over, let's review them:

Subject: What or whom the sentence is about. This person or thing will *do* or *be* something (contains a noun or pronoun).

Predicate: Word or words that tell what the subject is doing or being (contains the verb).

Creating simple sentences has become second nature to us and requires little thought on our part. We add a subject and a verb together and we automatically make the subject and the verb agree.

The **parent complains**.

> *The singular subject **parent** agrees with the verb **complains**. We would be able to tell if they did not agree simply by the way they sound.*

The **parents complains**.

> *This does not require understanding much about subject/verb agreement to understand that it is incorrect. But knowing why there is an agreement problem is required to correct some more complex sentences. Sounding right is not always the best way to judge a sentence.*

The problems regarding subject/verb agreement usually arise when sentences have compound subjects, phrases that intervene between the subject and the verb, or indefinite pronouns as the subject.

Anytime two or more nouns or pronouns make up the subject of a sentence and are connected by the word *and*, the subject becomes plural and will require a plural verb. If you remember back to your fifth grade math class, you will recall that the word *and* means to add. Similarly, in a sentence with *and* between the subjects, you are adding them together.

The **boy** and his 7-year-old **brother like** the same bikes.

If multiple subjects are separated by *or* or *nor*, the subjects are being separated (rather than added together) and the verb will agree with the noun or pronoun that appears closest to the verb in the sentence.

Neither the **fish** nor the **bird requires** much attention.

> *The nouns **fish** and **bird** are separated by the word nor. **Bird** is the closest noun to the verb, so the verb must agree with **bird**.*

The **bird requires**.

Neither the **fish** nor the **birds require** much attention.

> *If we make the word **birds** plural, then the verb must change to accommodate the plural subject.*

The **birds require**.

Understanding and identifying the subject and the verb in a sentence is necessary to ensure agreement between the two. If a phrase intervenes between the subject and the verb, make sure the verb agrees with the subject (and not with any part of the intervening phrase).

The **child**, along with his parents, **was introduced** to the school principal.

> ***Child**, not **parents**, is the subject of the sentence.*

The **child was introduced**.

Similarly, the subject of a sentence can **never** be in a prepositional phrase. (If you don't remember what a preposition or a prepositional phrase is, go back and review.) Prepositional phrases often follow the subject of a sentence, but don't get confused and try to make your verb agree with some part of the prepositional phrase. In fact, if you can mentally "cross out" the prepositional phrases, the subject of the sentence will be clear.

Excavation of the building site **was performed**.

> *Excavation*, *not building site, is the subject.* **Of the building site** *is a prepositional phrase and cannot contain the subject.*

Excavation was performed.

A **reading** of Shakespeare's works **reveals** much about the human condition.

> *The singular word* **reading** *is the subject. The subsequent prepositional phrase (**of Shakespeare's works**) lies between the subject and the verb and should be mentally "crossed out." The verb must agree with a singular subject.*

A **reading reveals**.

Challenge Box

Test yourself on these sentences. Which verb would agree with the subject(s) in the following sentences?

1. The woman, in addition to her roommates, (is/are) being moved into a new apartment.
2. Neither the lecture nor the grounding (has/have) changed the teenager's behavior.
3. A piece of the fractured eyeglasses (was/were) embedded in the boy's eye.

Subject/Verb Agreement with Pronouns

Perhaps the most difficult subject/verb agreement arrangement is when an indefinite pronoun is the subject of a sentence. An **indefinite pronoun** is a pronoun that replaces a noun without giving specific details about the noun it is replacing… it's indefinite. This ambiguity makes it hard to ensure agreement between the pronoun and the verb. Some indefinite pronouns are always singular, some are always plural, and some can be either, depending upon the context of the sentence.

SINGULAR	PLURAL	DEPENDS
each	several	some
no one	few	any
every one	both	most
anyone	many	all
someone		none
everyone		either…or
anybody		neither…nor
somebody		
everybody		
either		
neither		

The list is hard to memorize. Just remember, indefinite pronouns ending in *-one* or *-body* are always singular. The plural indefinite pronouns (several, many, few, etc.) sound plural so they are easier to recognize.

One of the flowers in the garden **(was/were) removed** because it was taking over the other flowers.

> *Which verb is correct?*

> *What is the subject? It can't be **flowers** or **garden** because they are each part of a prepositional phrase.*

> ***One** is the subject. It is singular. It requires a singular verb.*

One was removed.

One of the flowers in the garden **was removed** because it was taking over the other flowers.

Something in his eyes **(reveal/reveals)** his true feelings.

> *Which verb is correct?*

> *What is the subject? It can't be **eyes** because it is part of a prepositional phrase.*

> ***Something** is the subject. It is singular. It requires a singular verb.*

Something reveals.

Something in his eyes **reveals** his true feelings.

Those indefinite pronouns that can be either singular or plural seem to give people the most trouble. When using these pronouns, you must know what they are referring to and figure out if it is being used as a singular pronoun or a plural pronoun. The context of the sentence in which it is used will let you know if it is singular or plural.

Some of the buttons **were** loose.

> *In this sentence, **some** refers to the **buttons**, which is plural. Therefore, the verb must be plural.*

Some of the rash **was** fading.

> *In this sentence, **some** refers to the **rash**, which is singular. **Some** means part of the rash. Therefore, the verb must be singular.*

None of the boys **have** returned.

> *In this sentence, **none** refers to the boys, which is plural. Therefore, the verb must be plural.*

None of the pain **seems** acute.

> *In this sentence, **none** refers to the pain, which is singular. Therefore, the verb must be singular.*

A couple of phrases that often cause confusion are *the number of…* and *a number of…*. When these phrases contain the subject of a sentence, there are specific rules governing their use:

- When used as the subject, the phrase *The number of…* is singular
- When used as the subject, the phrase *A number of…* is plural

The number of pictures in the house is excessive.

A number of people arrive to watch the show.

Challenge Box

Test yourself on these sentences. Which verb would agree with the subject(s) in the following sentences?

1. Each of the essays (is/are) being examined.
2. Some of the people (has/have) already left.
3. A number of birds (was/were) scattered around the lawn.

Review: Subject/Verb Agreement

I. **MULTIPLE CHOICE.**
   Choose the best answer.

1. The prisoner, as mentioned in news reports, (○is, ○are) refusing to admit guilt.

2. The collection of stamps (○is, ○are) worth over $2,000.

3. The drawings of the surrounding landscape (○is, ○are) very detailed.

4. None of the bikes (○seems, ○seem) to be missing.

5. Flowers or chocolate (○appear, ○appears) to be a good solution for an apology present.

6. The angle of the buildings (○is, ○are) twisted in such a way as to create an optical illusion.

7. A number of popsicles (○was, ○were) mysteriously missing from the freezer.

8. Some of the damage (○appear, ○appears) to be from a previous flood.

9. The medication, in addition to the counseling, (○is, ○are) helping her overcome her grief.

10. Something in the kitchen (○are, ○is) causing a horrible smell.

11. None of the movies (○was, ○were) watched that night.

12. The forecast and the traffic (○appear, ○appears) clear.

13. All of the swelling in his knee (○disappear, ○disappears) with application of ice.

14. An agreement between all the friends (◯is, ◯are) easily reached.

15. Some of the memory loss from her father's Alzheimer's (◯seem, ◯seems) worse.

Pronoun Agreement

Luckily, once you have a good grasp of subject/verb agreement, pronoun agreement is a piece of cake. Because pronouns, by definition, take the place of nouns, they often occur in the same sentence as the nouns they replace. The noun that a pronoun refers to is known as its **antecedent**. A pronoun must agree with its antecedent in number (and gender, if applicable).

The **man** is going on vacation to **his** condo in January.

*The pronoun **his** refers to **man**, which is singular and, in this case, masculine.*

The woman's **parents** have a history of high cholesterol in **their** families.

*The pronoun **their** refers to **parents**, which is plural.*

While subjects and verbs must agree in number, pronouns and their antecedents must agree in number *and* gender.

Remember the rule governing compound subjects in subject/verb agreement? The rule applies to pronoun agreement as well. *And* between two nouns or pronouns makes the subject plural and *or* between two nouns separates them.

Bill's **wife and daughter** brought **their** gifts to him to the party.

*The pronoun **their** refers to his **wife** and his **daughter**, therefore it must be plural.*

Either the woman's **dog** or **cat** had sharpened **his** claws on the new couch.

*The pronoun **his** refers to either the **dog** or the **cat** (not both) so the pronoun must be singular.*

As with subject/verb agreement, a phrase intervening between the antecedent and the pronoun does not change the number or gender of the antecedent.

The **woman**, as well as her two best friends, went downtown to **her** favorite club.

*The pronoun **her** refers to the subject of the sentence (**woman**), so it must be singular.*

The sixth-grade **boys**, who all love sports, competed in **their** first baseball game today.

*The pronoun **their** refers to the subject of the sentence (**boys**), so it must be plural.*

Pronouns do not always have nouns as their antecedents. Sometimes a pronoun can refer to another pronoun. If the subject of a sentence is an indefinite pronoun, a pronoun somewhere else in the sentence may refer to it. Review the chart of indefinite pronouns from a couple of pages back if you need to.

Some of the students were excited to go on **their** choir tour.

*The pronoun **their** refers to the subject of the sentence (**some**), which is plural in this sentence. The prepositional phrase **of the students** cannot contain the subject.*

Some of the DVD was unwatchable because of the scratch on **its** surface.

*The pronoun **its** refers to the subject of the sentence (**some**), which is singular in this sentence. The prepositional phrase **of the DVD** cannot contain the subject.*

I. **MULTIPLE CHOICE.**
Choose the best answer.

1. The scars on his arm had (◯its, ◯their) origin in an automobile accident.

2. None of the book had any damage on (◯them, ◯it) from the flood.

3. The daughters of the old man said (◯their, ◯her) father had a history of smoking.

4. The cat was unharmed as it was removed from (◯their, ◯its) bed.

5. The car could not be found at (◯their, ◯its) owner's home.

6. The pain was mostly in his knee and ankle and (◯they, ◯it) got worse when he stood up.

7. The fireman's family came to (◯his, ◯their) work.

8. The region of the map indicated by the tour guides had lots of pencil markings on (◯them, ◯it).

9. The box was carried to the basement, and (◯they, ◯it) was opened using a knife.

10. The children were clearly upset by the storm, and (◯they, ◯it) were taken home.

Nominative Pronouns

Pronouns can be used in many places in a sentence and can perform several functions. They can appear as the subject of a sentence; when used this way, they are in the nominative case. The **nominative pronouns** are *I, you, he, she, it, we, they,* and *who*.

Without giving it any thought, you use these correctly nearly all the time.

She was brought to the zoo for her birthday.

***She** is the subject of the sentence. The pronoun is in the nominative case.*

They will call someone who can bring her to the airport.

> **They** is the subject of the sentence and **who** is the subject of the dependent clause **who can bring her to the airport**. These pronouns are in the nominative case.

The nominative case gives us problems when we have two pronouns or a noun and a pronoun together. If you say the sentence to yourself without the extra noun or pronoun, you will recognize the proper nominative case of the pronoun in question.

Incorrect: The accountant and her discussed the options for her financial portfolio.

> *If you drop **the accountant**, look what you are left with:*

Her discussed the options for her financial portfolio.

> *That is obviously not the right pronoun case.*

Correct: The accountant and she discussed the options for her financial portfolio.

The nominative case is used in comparisons that use the words *than* or *as*. Most comparisons leave words out at the end of the sentence (and if you add those words in, you can easily identify the proper pronoun case).

Incorrect: The man's wife is older than him.

> *In reality this sentence has been shortened. The word **is** has been left off the end of the sentence. If you add the word **is** to the end, you realize this is not the correct pronoun.*

Incorrect: The man's wife is older than him is.

Correct: The patient's wife is older than he.

Incorrect: His wife has not been a lawyer as long as him.

> *Again, this comparison in its complete form would have the word **has** at the end of it.*

Incorrect: His wife has not been a lawyer as long as him has.

Correct: His wife has not been a lawyer as long as he.

Objective Pronouns

Pronouns can also be used as the object (direct object or indirect object) of a verb or as the object of a preposition. Understandably, pronouns used in this way are said to be used in the **objective case**. The objective pronouns are *you, him, her, me, them, us, whom, and it.*

The teacher called me.
Me is the direct object of the verb **called**.

She wondered whom she should see about her car problems.
Whom is the direct object of the verb phrase **should see**.

When she arrived, the parking attendant gave her the keys to her car.
Her is the indirect object of the verb **gave**.

I offered his wife and him a brochure about the services we offer.
Him and wife are both indirect objects of the verb **offered**. *If you said this without the word* **wife**, *you would be able to tell that* **him** *is certainly the right pronoun choice.*

The woman would not reveal to whom the threats were intended.
Whom is the object of the preposition **to**.

Challenge Box

Test yourself on these sentences. Which pronouns should be used in the following sentences?

1. If we can meet with the teacher and (her/she), we can discuss ways to help raise her grades.
2. I discussed the option of a cruise with the woman and her husband, and she was more enthusiastic than (he/him).
3. The girl wondered from (whom/who) she may have gotten the flowers.

Possessive Pronouns

The final pronoun case is the **possessive case**. These are much simpler than the other cases and really require only your attention to the use (or lack of use) of the apostrophe.

As we mentioned in the Parts of Speech unit, personal pronouns and relative pronouns *do not* require apostrophes when used in the possessive case.

Hers is one of the clearest examples of a good presentation I have seen.

> *Hers* is a personal pronoun that is possessive.
>
> The team gave its report on this fiscal year.
>
> *Its* is a personal pronoun that is possessive.
>
> She could not remember whose book she had borrowed.
>
> *Whose* is a relative pronoun in the possessive case.

Indefinite pronouns in the possessive case *do* require apostrophes.

> She said **someone's** shoes were left on the stairs and caused her to trip.
>
> Her mother told me that she would not listen to **anybody's** offers for help.

I. MULTIPLE CHOICE.
Choose the best answer.

1. The car dealer asked his wife and (○ he, ○ him, ○ himself) to step into the office.

2. A person as young as (○ he, ○ him, ○ himself) should not have so many health problems.

3. The woman was asked if she was the one for (○ who, ○ whom, ○ whomever) the bullet was intended.

4. The boy said that (○ his, ○ him, ○ himself) parents were not aware of their activity.

5. No one is more aware of the seriousness of the issue than (○ her, ○ she, ○ herself).

6. The people from the dentist's office called (○ she, ○ herself, ○ her).

7. Between the father and (○ him, ○ he, ○ himself), there was already a complex relationship.

8. The clerk asked my partner and (○ I, ○ me, ○ we) to help carry boxes upstairs.

9. The woman's nine-year-old daughter is taller than (○ her, ○ she, ○ herself).

10. She did not know from (○ whom, ○ who, ○ whomever) the original phone call came.

Using the word(s) in the box, enter the appropriate term in the space provided. Terms may be used more than once.

1. When he arrived, he was as talkative as _____.

2. In an effort to minimize costs, the intern and _____ were asked to hand in their company-issued cell phones.

3. A fight between her boyfriend and _____ caused her initial injury.

4. The patient called for help from work, where _____ heavy lifting caused a debilitating pain in her lower back.

5. Although the dog was _____, she claimed to have never actually given it shots.

her
she
hers
herself

Modifier Placement

Perhaps nowhere is there more room for interpretive error on the part of the reader than when working with the placement (and misplacement) of modifiers.

A **modifier** is an adjective, adverb, phrase, or clause that acts as an adjective or an adverb—a modifier modifies something in the sentence. The importance of the **placement** of the modifier can be seen by looking at a couple of examples:

Taking several dog treats from the cupboard, the dog watched the woman carefully.

*The modifier is **Taking several dog treats from the cupboard**. The question must be asked, "WHO was taking dog treats from the cupboard?"*

*In this case, we hope it was the woman who was taking the dog treats out of the cupboard and not the dog. Notice the modifying phrase is right next to **the dog**. According to the placement of the modifier, it seems that the dog is taking dog treats from the cupboard.*

Running in a mad frenzy across the stage, the audience began to laugh.

Again, there is some confusion in this sentence. Did the audience run across the stage? Probably not.

How do we ensure that the modifier is saying exactly what we want it to say? Usually the placement of the modifier in the sentence can create clarity. When a sentence begins with a modifier, the thing (noun/pronoun) that immediately follows it should be the thing that is supposed to be modified. In our example sentences, this placement problem causes the confusion:

Taking several dog treats from the cupboard, the dog watched the woman carefully.

*In this sentence, the modifier is modifying **the dog** because it is the thing (noun) that immediately follows the modifying phrase.*

This confusion can be alleviated by changing the sentence and the placement of the modifier.

The dog watched **the woman** carefully **as she took several dog treats from the cupboard**.

This is much better. There is no doubt who was watching carefully and who was taking the dog treats from the cupboard.

Modifier Clarity

In an effort to simplify the modifier rules, we will list the most important ones here and give examples of each.

Modifiers at the beginning of a sentence

Make sure a modifier at the beginning of a sentence refers to the thing that comes right after it in the sentence.

Incorrect: Though legally blind, the construction site is not a hazardous place for the man.

Correct: Though he is legally blind, the man does not find the construction site hazardous.

OR

Correct: Though the man is legally blind, the construction site does not pose a hazard for him.

Modifier proximity to modified words

Place modifiers logically next to the word(s) they modify.

Incorrect: The man was driving his yellow sports car while talking on the phone at 85 miles per hour.

Correct: The man was driving his yellow sports car at 85 miles per hour while talking on the phone.

Limiting modifiers

Limiting modifiers should always go directly in front of the word(s) they modify. Limiting modifiers are *only, not, nearly, hardly, almost, just, merely, simply, even*.

Incorrect: The woman nearly had four beers.

*In this sentence, the placement of the word **nearly** implies that the woman narrowly escaped having four beers.*

Correct: The woman had nearly four beers.

*In this sentence, the placement of the word **nearly** explains that the woman had almost four beers.*

Split infinitives

Infinitives are created by placing the word *to* in front of a main verb (to walk, to laugh, to drive). Do not split up infinitives with long, intrusive modifiers. It will create an awkward sentence.

Incorrect: The man planned to, with the help of his trainer, complete a marathon that spring.

*The infinitive **to complete** is split by a long intervening phrase and the sentence becomes quite awkward.*

Correct: The man, with the help of his trainer, planned to complete a marathon that spring.

I. MULTIPLE CHOICE.
In the following exercises, there are two sentences. Select the one that has the correct use of modifiers.

1. ○ The family has been on vacation for a week at the beach and are ready to come home.
   ○ On vacation, the family has been at the beach for a week and are ready to come home.

2. ○ Expecting the worst, the woman was surprised to see she had received an interview request through e-mail.
   ○ Expecting the worst, the e-mail was a surprising interview request to the woman.

3. ○ The woman was taken to the room with a wheelchair.
   ○ The woman was taken in a wheelchair to the examining room.

4. ○ Describing the climb as long and arduous, the guide explained that the trip is not for the faint of heart.
   ○ Describing the climb as long and arduous, the trip is not for the faint of heart, according to the guide.

5. ○ After receiving explanations of the terms and conditions, the man signed the contract.
   ○ After receiving explanations of the terms and conditions, the contract was signed.

6. ○ After the rehearsal, the girl was barely able to recite her lines with any help.
   ○ After the rehearsal, the girl was able to recite her lines with barely any help.

7. ○ The woman arrived with extreme pain in her workplace.
   ○ The woman arrived at her workplace in extreme pain.

8. ○ Playful and energetic, the dog seemed to be in good spirits.
   ○ Playful and energetic, she thought the dog was in good spirits.

9. ○ The woman with six children said she wanted to travel.
   ○ The woman said she wanted to travel with six children.

10. ○ As a young child, the psychiatrist had helped the boy overcome the feelings from his parent's divorce.
    ○ The psychiatrist had helped the boy as a young child overcome the feelings from his parent's divorce.

Parallel Structure

It has often been said that good writing is a mix of art and science. While you do not need the artistic abilities to write a great piece of prose, you do have to make sure that what you write is precise. So, your writing must be good writing.

One of those rules that seems more science than art that governs the English language is that of parallel structure. Parallel means the same thing in writing that it does in geometry: having the same course, direction, nature, or tendency. You can look at two lines and tell if they are parallel or not almost immediately. With writing, of course, it takes a little closer inspection. Parallelism means that you have consistency in the patterns and structures in your writing—usually this means using similar forms of words, phrases, or clauses.

Incorrect: The table was washed, the plates were set, and they put the food on the table.

We have three clauses in this sentence that need to be parallel. To make them parallel, they must be written in the same form. When you separate them, you can see that they are not in the same form:

The table was washed
The plates were set
And they put the food on the table.

The structure that was set up by the first two clauses—the + noun + verb phrase—is broken by the last clause. It can easily be corrected by putting it into the same pattern.

Correct: The table was washed, the plates were set, and the food was put on the table.

To maintain parallelism in a sentence, do not mix forms: If you use the infinitive form (*to* + verb), use it throughout. If you use the gerund form (*ing* ending on a verb), use it throughout.

Incorrect: The woman was asked to close her eyes, to breathe calmly, and report any thoughts that came up.

Correct: The woman was asked to close her eyes, to breathe calmly, and to report any thoughts that came up.

Incorrect: He saw a woman running from the scene, a man waving a gun, and a police officer tackle the man.

Correct: He saw a woman running from the scene, a man waving a gun, and a police officer tackling the man.

When clauses are used in a sentence, their use must continue throughout (if in a series).

Incorrect: Her mother told her that she should get some rest, that she should drink plenty of fluids, and to use ice as needed.

Correct: Her mother told her that she should get some rest, that she should drink plenty of fluids, and that she should use ice as needed.

OR (if you want it less wordy)

Correct: Her mother told her that she should get some rest, drink plenty of fluids, and use ice as needed.

If the lists are part of a sentence (as opposed to a vertical numbered list), parallelism should be maintained unless your account instructions say otherwise.

Incorrect: She says that the following activities are her favorite: swimming, running, and doing dance.

Correct: She says that the following activities are her favorite: swimming, running, and dancing.

I. **TRUE/FALSE.**
Mark the following true if the sentence has parallel structure or false if there is a parallel structure error(s).

1. The man reported that he tripped over the step, grabbed the railing, and fell down three stairs.
   ○ true
   ○ false

2. The man was congenial, alert, and the kind of person who does mind questions.
   ○ true
   ○ false

3. She reported the following symptoms: dizziness, headache, needing to urinate.

   ○ true
   ○ false

4. A financial analysis, tax preparation, and business consultation were performed by the accounting firm.

   ○ true
   ○ false

5. The cake was prepared, the candles were lit, and I set the cake on the table.

   ○ true
   ○ false

6. The old man was helped to his feet, given water, and they drove him home.

   ○ true
   ○ false

7. He is upset, is trying to calm himself down, and is leaving the situation.

   ○ true
   ○ false

8. Glue was applied to the paper, glitter was sprinkled on top, and beads were placed among the glitter.

   ○ true
   ○ false

9. He poured water into some buckets, into a few pots, and the large barrel in the backyard.

   ○ true
   ○ false

10. The wall was scrubbed, sanded, and paint was applied.

   ○ true
   ○ false

Unit 7
Commonly Misspelled Words

Commonly Misspelled Words – Introduction

The following pages consist of a list of frequently misspelled words. The list has been broken up into manageable exercise sets to make learning them easier. It is important to note that this list has been compiled from a number of sources, but it is by no means exhaustive. These are words which you should know. If you are completely unaware of the meaning of any of these terms, please look up the word in a regular dictionary or an online dictionary. Familiarize yourself with the terms and complete the appropriate exercises.

Again, the content is broken down into alphabetical groupings. As with other material in this training program, it is easier to learn and memorize the spelling of these terms with some hands-on practice. So, here we go!

Commonly Misspelled Words (A)

I. **FILL IN THE BLANK.**
   Spelling and typing practice. Simply enter the given word in the space provided.

1. absence _____ 2. absorption _____

3. accessible _____ 4. accidentally _____

5. accommodate _____ 6. accommodation _____

7. accumulate _____ 8. accumulation _____

9. achieve _____ 10. advantageous _____

11. affect _____ . 12. all right _____

II. MULTIPLE CHOICE.
In the following exercise, there is a list of four possible spellings for a given word. Select the one that is spelled correctly.

1. ○ advantagous
   ○ advantagious
   ○ advantageous
   ○ advantajeous

2. ○ achieve
   ○ acheive
   ○ acheeve
   ○ acchieve

3. ○ abcense
   ○ absense
   ○ absence
   ○ abscence

4. ○ accessable
   ○ acessible
   ○ accesible
   ○ accessible

5. ○ all right
   ○ alright
   ○ allright
   ○ al right

6. ○ absorpsion
   ○ absorption
   ○ absarption
   ○ absroption

7. ○ accommadate
   ○ acommodate
   ○ accomadate
   ○ accommodate

8. ○ acidentally
   ○ accidentaly
   ○ accidentally
   ○ accadentally

9. ○ affect
   ○ afect
   ○ effeict
   ○ effact

10. ○ accumalate
    ○ acumulate
    ○ accummulate
    ○ accumulate

Commonly Misspelled Words (A–B)

I. **FILL IN THE BLANK.**
   Enter the given word in the space provided.

1. alignment _____   2. a lot _____

3. ambience _____   4. analyze _____

(ambiance is also an acceptable spelling)   5. asterisk _____

6. believe _____   7. believer _____

8. believing _____   9. belligerent _____

10. beneficial _____   11. boutonniere _____

12. business _____

II. MULTIPLE CHOICE.
In the following exercise, there is a list of four possible spellings for a given word. Select the one that is spelled correctly.

1. ○ annalyze
   ○ analyze
   ○ analize
   ○ anolyze

2. ○ alot
   ○ allot
   ○ a lot
   ○ a lott

3. ○ ambience
   ○ ambiense
   ○ ambiantce
   ○ ambianse

4. ○ alinement
   ○ alignement
   ○ allignment
   ○ alignment

5. ○ asterix
   ○ asterisk
   ○ astrix
   ○ astrisk

6. ○ beleive
   ○ believe
   ○ bellieve
   ○ belleive

7. ◯ boutinniere
   ◯ boutonniere
   ◯ bouttoniere
   ◯ bouttiniere

8. ◯ belligerent
   ◯ balligerant
   ◯ belligerant
   ◯ beligerant

Commonly Misspelled Words (C)

I. **FILL IN THE BLANK.**
   Enter the given word in the space provided.

1. category _____   2. challenge _____

3. changeable* _____   4. collateral _____

5. comparative _____   6. concede _____

7. congratulations _____ 8. connoisseur _____

9. cooperate _____   10. correlate _____

11. corroborate _____   12. criticism _____

This is one of a class of words, mostly ending in "ge" or "ce" that do not drop the "e" because to do so would make the consonant sound of the "c" or "g" turn hard. Thus, "changeable" without the "e" becomes "changable"—with a hard "g." The same thing is true of "knowledgeable." An example of the same principle with a "ce" word is "noticeable." Without the "e," it would be read and pronounced "notikable."

II. MULTIPLE CHOICE.

In the following exercise, there is a list of four possible spellings for a given word. Select the one that is spelled correctly.

1. ○ changeable
   ○ changable
   ○ changiable
   ○ changible

2. ○ concead
   ○ consede
   ○ concede
   ○ concide

3. ○ corroborate
   ○ corroberate
   ○ coroborate
   ○ corraborate

4. ○ category
   ○ catagory
   ○ cattegory
   ○ cattagory

5. ○ comparitive
   ○ comparative
   ○ comparetive
   ○ comparrative

6. ○ chalenge
   ○ chalange
   ○ challange
   ○ challenge

7. ○ congratulations
   ○ congradulations
   ○ congrattulations
   ○ congradualations

8. ○ connisere
   ○ conniseure
   ○ connosseure
   ○ connoisseur

9. ○ callateral
   ○ collateral
   ○ colateral
   ○ calateral

10. ○ cooperate
    ○ cooparate
    ○ cooperrate
    ○ copperate

Commonly Misspelled Words (D)

I. FILL IN THE BLANK.
Enter the given word in the space provided.

1. deceive _____

2. definitely _____

3. description _____

4. desperate _____

5. differentiate _____

6. differentiation _____

7. disappear _____

8. disappearance _____

9. disastrous _____

10. discernible _____

11. dissatisfied _____

12. dominant _____

II. MULTIPLE CHOICE.

In the following exercise, there is a list of four possible spellings for a given word. Select the one that is spelled correctly.

1. ○ definitly
   ○ definately
   ○ definitely
   ○ definitivly

2. ○ dominant
   ○ dominent
   ○ dominint
   ○ domanint

3. ○ disapearance
   ○ disappearance
   ○ dissapearence
   ○ disappearence

4. ○ disernible
   ○ discernable
   ○ disernable
   ○ discernible

5. ○ deceive
   ○ decieve
   ○ deiceve
   ○ diceive

6. ○ differentation
   ○ diferentiation
   ○ differantiation
   ○ differentiation

7. ○ disasterous
   ○ disastrous
   ○ dissastrous
   ○ disastrus

8. ◯ desparate
   ◯ desperete
   ◯ desperate
   ◯ despirate

9. ◯ discription
   ◯ description
   ◉ descreption
   ◯ descriptoin

10. ◯ dissatisfied
    ◯ disatisfied
    ◯ dissatesfied
    ◯ dissatisfyed

Commonly Misspelled Words (E)

I. **FILL IN THE BLANK.**
   Enter the given word in the space provided.

1. effect _____

2. eligible _____

3. embarrassing _____

4. equivalent _____

5. especially _____

6. exacerbate _____

7. exacerbation _____

8. exaggerate _____

9. exaggeration _____

10. exercise _____

11. existence _____

12. extraordinary _____

II. MULTIPLE CHOICE.
In the following exercise, there is a list of four possible spellings for a given word. Select the one that is spelled correctly.

1. ○ equivalent
   ○ equivelant
   ○ equivelent
   ○ equivalant

2. ○ exaserbate
   ○ exascerbate
   ○ excacerbate
   ○ exacerbate

3. ○ extradinary
   ○ extrordinary
   ○ extraordinary
   ○ extraordiniary

4. ○ exxageration
   ○ exaggeration
   ○ exageration
   ○ exsaggeration

5. ○ embarasing
   ○ embarrasing
   ○ embarassing
   ○ embarrassing

6. ○ exercise
   ○ excercise
   ○ ecsercise
   ○ exsercise

7. ○ existance
   ○ excsistance
   ○ excistance
   ○ existence

8. ○ especially
   ○ expecially
   ○ exspecially
   ○ especialy

Commonly Misspelled Words (F–I)

I. **FILL IN THE BLANK.**
   Enter the given word in the space provided.

1. financially _____   2. fluctuate _____

3. fluctuation _____   4. forty _____

5. grammar _____   6. grievous _____

7. harassment _____   8. hygiene _____

9. illegible _____   10. incidentally _____

11. independent _____   12. indispensable _____

II. **MULTIPLE CHOICE.**
   In the following exercise, there is a list of four possible spellings for a given word. Select the one that is spelled correctly.

1. ○ forty
   ○ fourty
   ○ forrty
   ○ forety

2. ○ indispensable
   ○ indespensible
   ○ indispensible
   ○ indespensable

3. ○ gramar
   ○ grammar
   ○ gramer
   ○ grammer

4. ○ fluctuation
   ○ fluchuation
   ○ fluctution
   ○ flutuation

5. ○ grievous
   ○ grievious
   ○ grevious
   ○ greivious

6. ○ hygene
   ○ hygiene
   ○ higyene
   ○ hygeine

7. ○ harasment
   ○ harrasment
   ○ harassment
   ○ harrassment

8. ○ independant
   ○ independent
   ○ imdependent
   ○ independant

9. ○ incidently
   ○ insidentaly
   ○ incidentally
   ○ insidentally

10. ○ illegible
    ○ ilegible
    ○ illegable
    ○ ilegable

Commonly Misspelled Words (I–N)

I. FILL IN THE BLANK.
Enter the given word in the space provided.

1. insistent _____

2. irrelevant _____

3. irresistible _____

4. judgment* _____

5. knowledgeable _____

6. labeled _____

7. labeling _____

8. legitimate _____

9. leisure** _____

10. maintenance _____

11. necessary _____

12. negligence _____

This is the preferred spelling of judgment. The spelling "judgement" is marginally acceptable.

**This one is confusing because most Americans pronounce it "leezure" while the traditional English pronunciation is "layzure," which follows the pronunciation rule for other words like "neighbor" and "weigh."*

II. MULTIPLE CHOICE.
In the following exercise, there is a list of four possible spellings for a given word. Select the one that is spelled correctly.

1. ○ neglagence
   ○ negligance
   ○ negligence
   ○ negligince

2. ○ judgment
   ○ judgement
   ○ jugment
   ○ jugement

3. ○ necesary
   ○ necessary
   ○ neccesary
   ○ necassary

4. ◯ incistent
    ◯ insistent
    ◯ incistant
    ◯ insistant

5. ◯ knowledgable
    ◯ knowlidgable
    ◯ knowledgible
    ◯ knowledgeable

6. ◯ legimate
    ◯ legitimate
    ◯ legitamite
    ◯ legittamite

7. ◯ irresistable
    ◯ iresistable
    ◯ irresistible
    ◯ iresistible

8. ◯ leisure
    ◯ liesure
    ◯ leizure
    ◯ liezure

9. ◯ labelled
    ◯ labeld
    ◯ labeled
    ◯ labled

10. ◯ maintenance
    ◯ mantenance
    ◯ maintinance
    ◯ maintanance

Commonly Misspelled Words (N–P)

I. **FILL IN THE BLANK.**
   Enter the given word in the space provided.

1. noticeable _____

2. occasion _____

3. occasionally _____

4. occur _____

5. occurrence _____

6. occurring _____

7. omission _____

8. opinion _____

9. parallel _____

10. perseverance _____

11. persistent _____

12. plural _____

II. **MULTIPLE CHOICE.**
   In the following exercise, there is a list of four possible spellings for a given word. Select the one that is spelled correctly.

1. ○ plural
    ○ plurral
    ○ pleural
    ○ pleral

2. ○ occuring
    ○ occurring
    ○ ocurring
    ○ ocuring

3. ○ noticable
    ○ notisable
    ○ noticeable
    ○ noticible

4. ○ parallel
    ○ paralel
    ○ parellel
    ○ parellal

5. ○ ommission
   ○ omission
   ○ ommision
   ○ omision

6. ○ persistent
   ○ persistant
   ○ persestant
   ○ persisstent

7. ○ persaverance
   ○ perseverence
   ○ perserverance
   ○ perseverance

8. ○ occasionally
   ○ occassionally
   ○ occasionaly
   ○ ocassionaly

Commonly Misspelled Words (P–R)

I. **FILL IN THE BLANK.**
   Enter the given word in the space provided.

1. possesses _____

2. precede* _____

3. preferable _____

4. preference _____

5. preferred _____

6. proceed* _____

7. procedure _____

8. pronunciation _____

9. questionnaire _____

10. receive _____

11. recommend _____

12. recur _____

*To effectively differentiate between these two terms, it is necessary for you to understand their meanings.
precede: to be, come, or go before in time, place, rank, etc.
proceed: to continue on, especially after stopping; to come forth or issue from

II. MULTIPLE CHOICE.
In the following exercise, there is a list of four possible spellings for a given word. Select the one that is spelled correctly.

1. ○ reccomend
   ○ reccommend
   ○ recommend
   ○ recomend

2. ○ recieve
   ○ receive
   ○ reseive
   ○ resieve

3. ○ posesses
   ○ poseses
   ○ possessess
   ○ possesses

4. ○ questionaire
   ○ questionare
   ○ questionnaire
   ○ questioniare

5. ○ pronunciation
   ○ pronounciation
   ○ proununciation
   ○ pronuncation

6. ○ preferable
   ○ preferrable
   ○ preferrible
   ○ preferible

7. ○ referrence
   ○ refference
   ○ reference
   ○ referance

8. ○ preferred
   ○ perferred
   ○ prefered
   ○ perfered

Commonly Misspelled Words (R–S)

I. **FILL IN THE BLANK.**
   Enter the given word in the space provided.

1. recurring _____

2. referable** _____

3. reference** _____

4. referred** _____

5. referring** _____

6. repetition _____

7. resistance _____

8. resistant _____

9. rhythm _____

10. rhythmical _____

11. seize* _____

12. separate*** _____

As with "leisure," this term breaks the "i" before "e" rule. It was likely pronounced "sayze" in Middle English.

**Note that words with the roots "prefer" and "refer" require the single consonant when the accent is on the first syllable (PREFerable) and the double consonant when the accent is on the second syllable (preFERred).*

***Remember that there is "a rat" in the middle of the word **separate**, and you'll always get it right.*

II. MULTIPLE CHOICE.

In the following exercise, there is a list of four possible spellings for a given word. Select the one that is spelled correctly.

1. ○ resistance
   ○ resistence
   ○ resistense
   ○ resistanse

2. ○ rhytham
   ○ rhithm
   ○ rhythm
   ○ rhythem

3. ○ refered
   ○ referred
   ○ reffered
   ○ refferred

4. ○ repatition
   ○ repitition
   ○ repittition
   ○ repetition

5. ○ sepirate
   ○ seperate
   ○ separrate
   ○ separate

6. ○ reoccuring
   ○ reccurring
   ○ recurring
   ○ recuring

7. ○ resistent
   ○ resistant
   ○ ressistant
   ○ ressistent

Commonly Misspelled Words (S–Z)

I. FILL IN THE BLANK.
Enter the given word in the space provided.

1. superintendent _____   2. supersede _____

3. supposedly _____   4. surprise _____

5. their* _____   6. there* _____

7. they're* _____   8. vacuum** _____

9. versus*** _____   10. vicious _____

11. your**** _____   12. you're**** _____

*These three words are pronounced exactly the same. You should already be familiar with their meanings, but for review:

"Their" is simply a possessive pronoun. "It is their piano."

"There" is an adverb. "We were on our way there when the car broke down."

"They're" is a contraction of "they are." "They're likely to quit after this."

**Think of this as vac-u-um, with three syllables rather than vac-yume with only two syllables. It may help you to remember how to spell it.

***This is not to be confused with "verses," the units of a poem or song (which you will probably never see in a letter to a client). Instead, you might say, "Looking at Blair & Co. versus Designers Inc., we would choose Blair & Co."

****These words are also pronounced the same. For your review:

"Your" is a possessive pronoun. "It's all in your head."

"You're" is the contraction for "you are." "You're my best friend."

II. MULTIPLE CHOICE.

In the following exercise, there is a list of four possible spellings for a given word. Select the one that is spelled correctly.

1. ○ vacuum
   ○ vacum
   ○ vacume
   ○ vacume

2. ○ viscious
   ○ viscous
   ○ vicious
   ○ visious

3. ○ versis
   ○ versus
   ○ versise
   ○ verssus

4. ○ superseed
   ○ superceed
   ○ supercede
   ○ supersede

5. ○ suposedly
   ○ suposably
   ○ supposedly
   ○ supossedly

6. ○ surprize
   ○ surprise
   ○ suprize
   ○ suprise

7. ◯ superintendent
   ◯ supraintendant
   ◯ superintendant
   ◯ superintandent

8. ◯ thier
   ◯ thare
   ◯ their
   ◯ theyre

Answer Key

Parts of Speech

Nouns and Pronouns

1. **She** and **you** are personal pronouns and **what** is an interrogative pronoun.
2. **Everyone** is an indefinite pronoun and **her** is a possessive pronoun.
3. **These** is a demonstrative pronoun.
4. **That** is a relative pronoun that links the dependent clause **that landed here** to the word **plane**. **Its** is a possessive pronoun.
5. **Nobody** is an indefinite pronoun. **We** is a personal pronoun. **That** is a relative pronoun.

Adjectives

I. MULTIPLE CHOICE.

1. pronoun
2. adjective - store
3. noun
4. adjective - mall
5. noun
6. pronoun
7. adjective - son
8. noun
9. pronoun
10. adjective - chili dogs
11. noun
12. adjective - car
13. adjective - car
14. noun
15. adjective - chest
16. pronoun
17. adjective - chest
18. noun
19. adjective - tabletop

Verbs

1. **Will call** is a compound verb and it shows action.
2. **Received** is an action verb.
3. **Does have** is a compound verb showing action. **Will send** is a compound verb and it shows action.
4. **Appeared** is a linking verb that shows his state of being (oriented). **Spoke** is an action verb.
5. **Looks** is a linking verb expressing state of being (good). **Will follow up** is a compound verb showing action. **Change** is an action verb.

Adverbs in Action

I. MULTIPLE CHOICE.

1. immediately
2. normally
3. somewhat
4. unusually
5. yearly

II. FILL IN THE BLANK.

1. leave
2. went
3. had watched
4. deteriorated
5. misjudged

Review: Parts of Speech

1. adjective - boy
2. adverb
3. noun
4. noun
5. verb
6. adjective - seashell
7. verb
8. noun
9. pronoun
10. adverb
11. verb
12. adverb
13. adverb
14. noun
15. adjective - sister
16. pronoun
17. pronoun
18. verb
19. adverb
20. pronoun
21. verb
22. adjective - seashell
23. verb
24. adverb
25. noun

Prepositions

CHALLENGE BOX.

1. on the corner
2. over the window
3. For the first time, by himself
4. on the couch, to them all
5. down the street

I. TRUE/FALSE.

1. false
2. true
3. false
4. true
5. true
6. true
7. false
8. true
9. false
10. false

Conjunctions

CHALLENGE BOX.

1. **Or** is a coordinating conjunction.
2. **Neither...nor** is a correlative conjunction. **Yet** is a coordinating. **And** is a coordinating conjunction.
3. **And** is a coordinating conjunction.

I. PARTS OF SPEECH.

1. and
2. or
3. none
4. but
5. and
6. none
7. and, and
8. none
9. none
10. but

Sentences

Sentence Fragments

I. MULTIPLE CHOICE.

1. missing predicate
2. missing predicate
3. has subject and predicate, but is an incomplete thought
4. missing subject
5. has subject and predicate, but is an incomplete thought
6. missing subject
7. missing subject
8. missing predicate
9. has subject and predicate, but is an incomplete thought
10. missing subject

Fixing Fragments

I. MULTIPLE CHOICE.

1. The dinner was ready.
2. He was asked to set the table.
3. Dinner was served when they had finished preparing it.
4. The family ate together.
5. His father's favorite was the soup.
6. After dinner it was time for dessert.
7. His mother had made his favorite dessert.
8. He shouted with delight when his mother brought it in.

Run-Ons and Comma Splices

I. MULTIPLE CHOICE.

1. run-on
2. complete sentence
3. complete sentence
4. comma splice
5. comma splice
6. complete sentence
7. run-on
8. run-on
9. complete sentence
10. comma splice

Punctuation

Commas with Independent Clauses and Series

I. PROOFREADING.

1. The girl was very eclectic in her music tastes , but she preferred to listen to classical music.
2. Some of her favorite composers were Bach , Mozart , and Chopin.
3. She enjoyed playing classical music on the piano , and she often bought new music to learn.
4. She often went to concerts , recitals , and performances.
5. Her favorite instruments were the violin and piano and harp.

Commas with Introductions

CHALLENGE BOX.

1. After a long and very intense exercise session, she felt as if her heart were pounding too hard to be healthy.
   After a long and very intense exercise session is a long prepositional phrase so it would have a comma after it.
2. Since she didn't want to leave her cat home alone, she took him on vacation with her.
   Since she didn't want to leave her cat home alone is an introductory clause.
3. Preparing for her wedding, she went to an expensive salon.
   Preparing for her wedding is an introductory phrase.

Commas with Nonessential Elements

I. MULTIPLE CHOICE.

1. For now he decided not to move out of his apartment.
2. Because she hadn't eaten enough that day, she felt weak.
3. Because he was out of the country, he missed his cousin's wedding.
4. After she was satisfied with the wrapping, she was ready to give her husband his birthday present.
5. The cars that were new were placed at the front display of the car lot.
6. The dog, a six-year-old cocker spaniel, bounded up to its owner in excitement.
7. The child was found to be happy, not to mention healthy, when he spent more of his time running around outside.
8. A friendly and confident person, she was a good choice for the prom queen.
9. The man had a bookshelf with no books in it.
10. Between you and me, I don't think I would have worn pants to a party like this.

Troublesome Comma Rules

I. MULTIPLE CHOICE.

1. The boat was prepped for a long, enjoyable ride.
2. The four friends climbed aboard and sat down.
3. They were ready to go; however, the boat needed extra gas.
4. Finally, the boat took off into the water, and the friends began to laugh.
5. The boat was fast, and the cool, refreshing wind blew through their hair.

Periods

I. PROOFREADING.

1. Dr . Johnson wanted to take a vacation . He called Mrs . Johnson to tell her they were going to Maine .
2. When he came home, his wife was thrilled . They scheduled the trip and packed .
3. The flight was not long , and then they arrived . They traveled to their bed and breakfast .
4. They enjoyed a meal of delicious clam chowder . That evening they walked along a beautiful beach .
5. After their trip was over , they were ready to go home . They were happy to have had such a great vacation .

Colons

I. MULTIPLE CHOICE.

1. He wanted two things: a puppy and a wagon.

2. After the accident the man had the following: blurred vision, headache, and a sore neck.

3. The doctor gave her his number one rule concerning prenatal care: You are no longer the most important person in your own life.

4. The woman had a special name for her two-year-old niece: The Tornado.

5. She has had no candy bars, peppermints, or other types of candy for days.

Parentheses

I. PROOFREADING.

1. Her favorite thing to do in her spare time was to ride motorcycles(~~On~~ **on** a dirt race track, I believe ~~.~~). She traveled around the country riding her motorcycle ~~[with~~ **(with** a team of other ~~racers.]~~ **racers).**

2. The man started having problems with his balance eight years ago .(It started after a concussion.)He got tired and lost his balance often when he exercised.(~~he~~ **He** had been running for years .)

Hyphens – Lesson 2

I. PROOFREADING.

1. She called her ~~exhusband~~ **ex-husband** to see if he was coming to pick up their ~~9 year old~~ **9-year-old** son.

2. He went in for a followup and discussed the ~~xray~~ **x-ray** with his doctor.

3. The ~~president elect~~ **president-elect** gave an inspiring speech.

4. She has a ~~3~~ **3-**, ~~5~~ **5-**, and ~~9 year old~~ **9-year-old** child at home.

Apostrophes – Lesson 1

CHALLENGE BOX.

1. **Purse's**. Since the purse is singular, you really don't need to think much…nearly all singular words use apostrophe s when they become possessive.

2. **Teachers'**. The word **teachers** is plural and ends in *s*, so it requires only an apostrophe.

Apostrophes – Lesson 2

I. MULTIPLE CHOICE.

1. men's
2. one's
3. Ross's
4. days'
5. father-in-law's
6. students'
7. mother and father's
8. children's
9. its
10. brother's

Quotation Marks

I. PROOFREADING.

1. She described the issue as **"** a confusion with the delivery of my ~~fees~~ **fees. "**

2. ~~Stop Stop~~ **" Stop! Stop!** You can ' t take my ~~purse~~ **purse! "** she screamed at the thief .

3. He described the color of the skin as **"** sea ~~green~~ **green. "**

4. When asked about the headache , she said ~~this~~ , **" This** is the worst pain I have ever ~~felt~~ **felt. "**

5. The boy repeatedly asked ~~when~~ , **" When** are we ~~leaving~~ **leaving? "**

Capitalization

Capitalization Rules 1–5

I. PROOFREADING.
1. ~~keep~~ **Keep** this in mind: ~~the~~ **The** only way in is through the front door.
2. The little girl is ~~Right Handed~~ **right handed**. ~~she~~ **She** has not had many blood draws in the left arm.
3. His health required the following rigorous diet: increased fiber, decreased dairy, and no sodas at all.
4. It was late when she arrived home. ~~the~~ **The** clock in her bedroom read 2:03.
5. ~~she~~ **She** had to buy the following ingredients at the store: milk, bread, and eggs.

Capitalization Rules 6–10

CHALLENGE BOX.
1. Once we get the results from Doctor Bateman, we may refer her to a pain clinic.
2. This patient suffered an injury to her femur during her work in the US Postal Service.
3. This patient will be seen by Cardiology immediately, and I will consult with Jared Decker, MD, FACC.
4. If we get the pulmonary tests back, we will have her follow up with East Wayne Pulmonary Center.

I. MULTIPLE CHOICE.
1. The consulting doctor ordered the patient to Radiology for an immediate x-ray.
2. At this time we will ask the patient to follow up with Dr. Alec at the podiatry clinic.
3. He stopped by the National Broadcasting Company's headquarters when he toured the city.
4. She was escorted to us from Early Dawn Mental Health by Officer Mason.
5. He filled out a worker's compensation claim when he was injured while working for the city.

Capitalization Rules 11–14

CHALLENGE BOX.
1. Tick-borne diseases like this are not uncommon in the North this time of year.
2. The patient has been exposed to severe acute respiratory syndrome, also known as SARS.
3. She is a Hispanic woman from a town east of Columbia, South Carolina.
4. If her progress continues, we will see her in July and then not again until fall.

I. TRUE/FALSE.
1. false
2. true
3. false
4. true
5. false

Agreement

Tense Agreement

I. TRUE/FALSE.

1.	false	2.	true
3.	false	4.	false
5.	true	6.	true
7.	false	8.	true
9.	false	10.	false

Subject/Verb Agreement

CHALLENGE BOX.

1. **Is** is the correct answer. **Woman** is the subject; **in addition to her roommates** is an intervening phrase and cannot contain the subject.
2. **Has** is the correct answer. **Grounding** is the subject closest to the verb, so the verb must agree with it.
3. **Was** is the correct answer. **Piece** is the subject; **of the fractured eyeglasses** is a prepositional phrase and cannot contain the subject.

Subject/Verb Agreement with Pronouns

CHALLENGE BOX.

1. **Is** is the correct answer. **Each** is the subject and is a singular pronoun; **of the essays** is a prepositional phrase and cannot contain the subject.
2. **Have** is the correct answer. **Some** is the subject. In this case it is referring to the **people** (which is plural). It means part of the people.
3. **Were** is the correct answer. **A number** is the subject and is plural when used this way.

Review: Subject/Verb Agreement

I. MULTIPLE CHOICE.

1.	is	2.	is
3.	are	4.	seem
5.	appear	6.	is
7.	were	8.	appears
9.	is	10.	is
11.	were	12.	appear
13.	disappears	14.	is
15.	seems		

Pronoun Agreement

I. MULTIPLE CHOICE.

1.	their	2.	it
3.	their	4.	its
5.	its	6.	it
7.	his	8.	it
9.	it	10.	they

Objective Pronouns

CHALLENGE BOX.

1. **Her** is the correct answer. **Her** is the object of the preposition **with**. If you said the sentence without the words **the teacher**, you would be able to choose the right pronoun easily.
2. **He** is the correct answer. The word **was** has been left off of the end of the sentence... *more enthusiastic than he was.*
3. **Whom** is the correct answer. If you were to restate the sentence, it would be, "She got the flowers from **him**." So, **whom** is the object of the preposition **from**.

Possessive Pronouns

I. MULTIPLE CHOICE.

1. him
2. he
3. whom
4. his
5. she
6. her
7. him
8. me
9. she
10. whom

II. FILL IN THE BLANK.

1. she
2. she
3. her
4. her
5. hers

Modifier Clarity

I. MULTIPLE CHOICE.

1. The family has been on vacation for a week at the beach and are ready to come home.
2. Expecting the worst, the woman was surprised to see she had received an interview request through e-mail.
3. The woman was taken in a wheelchair to the examining room.
4. Describing the climb as long and arduous, the guide explained that the trip is not for the faint of heart.
5. After receiving explanations of the terms and conditions, the man signed the contract.
6. After the rehearsal, the girl was able to recite her lines with barely any help.
7. The woman arrived at her workplace in extreme pain.
8. Playful and energetic, the dog seemed to be in good spirits.
9. The woman with six children said she wanted to travel.
10. The psychiatrist had helped the boy as a young child overcome the feelings from his parent's divorce.

Parallel Structure

I. TRUE/FALSE.

1. true
2. false
3. false
4. true
5. false
6. false
7. true
8. true
9. false
10. false

Commonly Misspelled Words

Commonly Misspelled Words (A)

II. MULTIPLE CHOICE.

1. advantageous
2. achieve
3. absence
4. accessible
5. all right
6. absorption
7. accommodate
8. accidentally
9. affect
10. accumulate

Commonly Misspelled Words (A–B)

II. MULTIPLE CHOICE.

1. analyze
2. a lot
3. ambience OR ambiance
4. alignment
5. asterisk
6. believe
7. boutonniere
8. belligerent

Commonly Misspelled Words (C)

II. MULTIPLE CHOICE.

1. changeable
2. concede
3. corroborate
4. category
5. comparative
6. challenge
7. congratulations
8. connoisseur
9. collateral
10. cooperate

Commonly Misspelled Words (D)

II. MULTIPLE CHOICE.

1. definitely
2. dominant
3. disappearance
4. discernible
5. deceive
6. differentiation
7. disastrous
8. desperate
9. description
10. dissatisfied

Commonly Misspelled Words (E)

II. MULTIPLE CHOICE.

1. equivalent
2. exacerbate
3. extraordinary
4. exaggeration
5. embarrassing
6. exercise
7. existence
8. especially

Commonly Misspelled Words (F–I)

II. MULTIPLE CHOICE.

1. forty
2. indispensable
3. grammar
4. fluctuation
5. grievous
6. hygiene
7. harassment
8. independent
9. incidentally
10. illegible

Commonly Misspelled Words (I–N)

II. MULTIPLE CHOICE.

1. negligence
2. judgment
3. necessary
4. insistent
5. knowledgeable
6. legitimate
7. irresistible
8. leisure
9. labeled
10. maintenance

Commonly Misspelled Words (N–P)

II. MULTIPLE CHOICE.

1. plural
2. occurring
3. noticeable
4. parallel
5. omission
6. persistent
7. perseverance
8. occasionally

Commonly Misspelled Words (P–R)

II. MULTIPLE CHOICE.

1. recommend
2. receive
3. possesses
4. questionnaire
5. pronunciation
6. preferable
7. reference
8. preferred

Commonly Misspelled Words (R–S)

II. MULTIPLE CHOICE.

1. resistance
2. rhythm
3. referred
4. repetition
5. separate
6. recurring
7. resistant

Commonly Misspelled Words (S–Z)

II. MULTIPLE CHOICE.

1. vacuum
2. vicious
3. versus
4. supersede
5. supposedly
6. surprise
7. superintendent
8. their